Studies in Ethics

edited by
Robert Nozick
Pellegrino University Professor
at Harvard University

A Garland Series

ETHICS AND EPISTEMOLOGY IN SEXTUS EMPIRICUS

TAD BRENNAN

GARLAND PUBLISHING, INC.
A MEMBER OF THE TAYLOR & FRANCIS GROUP
NEW YORK & LONDON/1999

Published in 1999 by
Garland Publishing Inc.
A Member of the Taylor & Francis Group
19 Union Square West
New York, NY 10003

10 9 8 7 6 5 4 3 2 1

Library of Congress Cataloging-in-Publication Data
Library of Congress-in-Publication Data is available
from the Library of Congress

Brennan, Tad
Ethics and epistemology in sextus empiricus / Tad Brennan
Includes bibliographical references and index.
ISBN: 0-8153-3659-4 (alk paper)

Printed on acid-free, 250-year-life paper
Manufactured in the United States of America

To my Parents,
Anne Searls Brennan
and James Gerard Brennan

Contents

Preface

I am grateful to Damon Zucca of the Garland Publishing, and to Robert Nozick, the editor of this series, for their invitation to reprint my doctoral dissertation. I am happy that, through their efforts, my work will find a larger audience.

This is not, of course, because I view the work that I did six years ago with unalloyed satisfaction or an uncritical eye. No scholar can read their own juvenalia without feeling its deficiencies, lamenting its shortcomings, and wishing it better.

But those deficiencies confessed, I believe that this book has a contribution to make to the debate, still as interesting now as six years ago, over how we should understand Sextus Empiricus. One of its five chapters has already had some exposure, having been printed twice as a free-standing piece (see bibliography for Brennan 1994 and 2000).[1] But a survey of the work on Sextus that is currently in print reveals a void to be filled, and my work goes some way towards filling it, when its answers are right. When its answers do not succeed, it still should act to call attention to the points that need addressing, and move discussion into new directions.

While I cannot undertake a full or authoritative survey of the work that has appeared since my dissertation, I have tried to update my bibliography by including the best and most significant pieces of recent work on Sextus and on related areas of Ancient

1 Accordingly, I here print as a replacement for the original Chapter 3 a version of that chapter updated and improved by the comments it has collected from editors, referees, and critics in its two published versions. The other portions of the dissertation are reprinted unchanged.

Skepticism. I would also like to say a few things about recent directions in Sextan studies.

The major trend discernible is the production of scholarly and philological commentaries on Sextus' treatises.[2] These have been of excellent quality, and from them I have learned much about individual passages in Sextus, about his sources, his linguistic usage, and sometimes about the details of particular arguments.

On larger issues, alas, there has been less progress. Hankinson 1995 deserves our thanks for attempting to paint with a broad brush. The detail work was deficient, however, and his book was roundly, and deservedly, criticized by Brittain 1997 and Fine 1996. Bett 1997 combines the excellent philological scholarship noted above with some less satisfactory proposals for grand interpretive strategies; I mention a few of my dissatisfactions in Brennan 1998c. This lack of new directions is best signalized by a recent anthology which reprints the articles of Barnes, Burnyeat and Frede.[3] These articles were already nearly a decade old when I was wrestling with them, and the fact that their authors could not think of anything new to add to the debate when it was nearly two decades old—neither any new thoughts of their own, nor any new articles to add to the original five—suggests that something is amiss. One can only hope that any similar anthology a decade from now will feature fresh titles, and I in particular hope that the publication of this present work will aid that process of refreshment—even if only by offering a fresh target for scholars to attack.

It is a topos in prefaces to attribute to one's teachers and benefactors the outstanding merits of the work in hand, while taking onto one's own shoulders its remaining weaknesses and flaws. As an historian of philosophy, I have always found this asymmetrical attribution quite baffling. Who supposes, of any historical pair of thinkers, that the elder passed on to the younger only truth, and that the younger acquired their errors only through their own efforts? We feel confident that Plato imbibed much knowledge from the Socratic fount; but equally confident that much of what is erroneous in Plato is an extension of his teacher's faulty ideas. We cannot imagine without laughter, a preface in which Malebranche

2 Spinelli 1995, as well as Bett 1997 and Blank 1998, the last two both under the aegis of the Clarendon Later Ancient Philosophers series.

3 Burnyeat and Frede 1997, which consists of Barnes 1983, Burnyeat 1980a, Burnyeat 1984, Frede 1979, and Frede 1984.

thanks Descartes for whatever is true in his *Recherche de la Verité*, while arrogating to himself creative responsibility for all its *erreurs*. When the impartial inheritance of both falsehood and truth is such an evident historical fact, its routine denial in prefaces must seem either an inexcusable lapse into ignorance, or an inexplicable recourse to legal fictions.

Should some reader in the centuries to come peruse this dissertation with a mind well-informed of academic matters in our time, they would have no hesitation in attributing both its strengths and weaknesses to the milieu from which it arose, namely, the Anglophone and Analytic revival of Ancient Greek philosophy in the second half of the century, whose leading figures were G. E. L. Owen, Gregory Vlastos, and Günther Patzig. Finer-grained knowledge of dates and places might steer them away from assuming any direct contact with those three scholars, and towards the influence of their students and colleagues, esp. John Cooper, M. M. McCabe, David Furley, Jonathan Barnes, Myles Burnyeat, and Michael Frede.

To Cooper, McCabe and Furley my debts are most diffuse and difficult to trace, though the general similarity of style and spirit would appear from a distance. Barnes and Burnyeat, as the reader will discover, did me the immense service of disagreeing with me on fundamental points, and graciously encouraged me to press my disagreements. Frede, finally, was my main source of insight and error. My views on Sextus came to differ from his on most of the central points; my position is sufficiently distinct that I have no hesitation in offering it to the world as an original contribution and an alternative to all the other intepretations of which I am aware. That said, however, it must also be said that most of what I got right in all this, as well as most of what I got wrong, and most of what I simply never saw needed to be addressed at all, is due to Michael Frede. I believe that will be the judgement of the ages, and given my belief, I must eschew the normal formulae of exculpation or make this preface paradoxical. And indeed, I have no qualms about sharing out among my elders the credit for my errors as well as for my accuracies, since my gratitude is also indifferent to truth-value; it was an honor to study with them, right or wrong, and I thank them for the privilege.

What even a very keen historian of our era might not be able to reconstruct from this document would be the quality of personal interactions that underlay its composition. Thus I should emphasize the deep satisfaction and joy that I have felt in the company of Ancient Philosophers, first as a student and now as a colleague. For a more detailed sketch of the personalities involved, I direct the reader to the original acknowledgement below, which I have retained unedited (again despite some feeling of embarrassment on rereading it). I only note, on this occasion, that my quip about "making a better life" with Liz Karns has since been made earnest in the person of a five-year old daughter, Alexandra Karns Brennan, and repeated without loss of novelty in the person of her two-year old brother, Lincoln Karns Brennan. I am grateful to them both for giving me the time to compose this preface. And as always, my deepest thanks go to Liz Karns.

Acknowledgments

"I have protracted my work until most of those whom I wished to please, have sunk into the grave, and success and miscarriage are empty sounds: I therefore dismiss it with frigid tranquillity, having little to fear or hope from censure or from praise." So wrote Johnson, ending the preface to his dictionary. The present work, though of much lighter moment, fills its author with a kindred heaviness; and this despite the fact that most of those whom I wished to please by its composition are still, the fates be praised, among the living. For it too was drawn out beyond all reason, and my case might be closer to Johnson's, if the protractive powers of medical science had not excelled my own. As it is, I am fortunate in being able to dedicate this work to two living parents; I began it wishing to please them, and now finish hoping for their praise.

After my parents, I want to thank the members of the Princeton Ancient Philosophy Program: David Furley, John Cooper, Michael Frede, and André Laks; and other members of the Classics Department: Robert Lamberton, T. James Luce, Richard Martin, and Ronnie Hanley. It also gives me great pleasure to mention two visitors to Princeton who made a great difference to my education: Myles Burnyeat, whose name occurs throughout this thesis, and M.M. McCabe, once my teacher and now my colleague. The confidence in me and in my work that she and Richard Sorabji expressed by asking me to join them at King's College, London came at a critical moment for my thesis and for my career, and I am immensely grateful to them both. To move from Princeton to King's is a coronation indeed.

I had other teachers at Princeton: my fellow graduate students. Among these I am happy to mention John Konkle, Charles Brittain, Hilary Mackie, Nancy Worman, Victoria Voytko, John Gutglueck, and Christian Perring.

Several people unconnected with Princeton nevertheless played an important role in my education. Pat Lambo, my psychotherapist, helped me to function through the recurrent depression and morbid hallucinations that have always plagued me as a student, and helped me pursue the god's injunction to know myself. My brother, James C. Brennan, is always a true friend, and was also my first teacher of Ancient Philosophy; I clearly remember him, when our combined years could not have reached a score, telling me that Aristotle was Plato's student, and Plato Socrates'; but that Socrates had not written anything. He has since taught me other lessons, no less accurate and vastly more valuable, about many things.

I save for last my dearest love and my deepest thanks, both of which are owed, and both of which I gladly give, to my wife Liz Karns. Teacher, colleague, fellow-student, friend, therapist, sibling—whatever others have been to me, she has been too; and many things no one else can be. First meeting me in the carefree years of my youthful employment, she saw me through the nine dark years of school, to my present state of even happier employment. Her strength, patience, humor, and joy have made my life immeasurably better; I look forward to making an even better life with her in the future.

Chapter One

Introduction

The aim of this thesis is to present an interpretation of the brand of skepticism represented in the writings of Sextus Empiricus. Currently, there is fairly broad agreement on how we should understand this form of skepticism (Sextan skepticism, as I shall call it); in the following chapters, I attempt to articulate an alternative view. The inspiration for this alternative view comes from some of Michael Frede's writings on Sextus, but I do not know what further relation there is between his views and the views I have arrived at in the course of this project. Its most succinct description, however, might be that it is an attempt to follow out the consequences of my interpretation of his interpretation of Sextus.[1]

In particular, it takes as its starting point such passages as PH II.246 and AM XI. 165, in which Sextus claims to live like other people, and to suspend judgment only about matters of abstract and technical philosophical debate.

> For it is, I think, sufficient to conduct one's life empirically and undogmatically in accordance with the rules and beliefs that are commonly accepted, suspending judgment regarding the statements derived from dogmatic subtlety and furthest removed from the usage of life. (PH II.246)[2]

1. I have also found views of Sextus that are congenial to my outlook, and roughly opposed to the critical consensus, in Hallie 1985, and in the articles of Robert Fogelin, as well as in a draft of an unpublished work on Sextus that he was kind enough to let me see. For which now see Fogelin 1994.

> ... the Skeptic does not live according to philosophical argument (for so far as that goes we are inactive), but is able to choose some things and avoid others. (AM XI.165)

Generally such passages as this are taken as evidence that Sextus had a very complicated stance towards practical activities and the cognitive processes involved in them. For it is taken as a given that the skeptic cannot have the full range of ordinary beliefs; and yet beliefs that are limited to how things appear to one do not seem adequate for most practical activities. So the challenge, as most interpreters see it, is to articulate a middle course between ordinary belief and mere reports of sense-data—an attenuated and weakened sort of cognitive attitude that could nevertheless underpin a life in some way described as "in accordance with" normal beliefs.

But it seemed to me worthwhile to make the experiment of supposing that the skeptic's cognitive attitudes are really no different from ordinary beliefs at all. This heterodox supposition then brings in its train other divergences from the standard view. For changing our view about the skeptic's beliefs naturally requires us

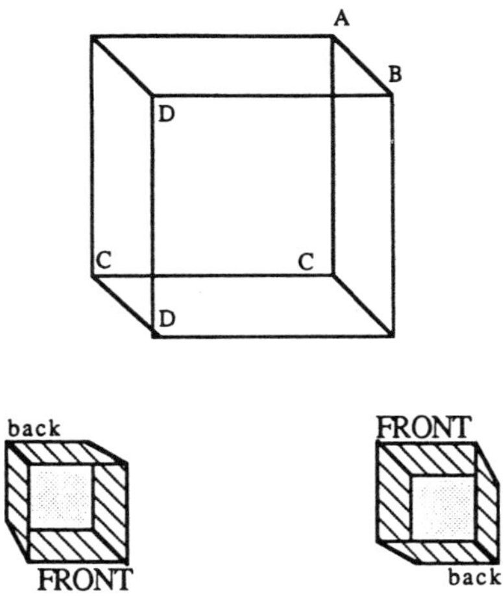

2. All translations are based on, and sometimes merely reproduce, those of Bury 1933. I used that as a clumsy but uncontroversial touchstone, wishing to avoid the under-handed importation of tendentious interpretations via idiosyncratic translations. My thought was that if I could make my points merely with the aid of Bury's English, then no one could accuse me of cutting my translation to suit my views. As it happened, I was pressed by David Sedley, who refereed Brennan 1994, to update and improve Bury to modern standards here and there. But I hope I have still chosen renderings that do not prejudge the important issues.

to review other connected areas, such as suspension, ataraxia, and so on, and to make adjustments in our view of them.

Although the alternative that I shall present differs from the standard view at a number of crucial points, it is, in another sense, nearly isomorphic to it in its overall structure. Indeed, the similarity of structure arises exactly because the disagreements are systematic;[3] and this creates peculiar difficulties of exposition. The case might be compared to the familiar phenomenon of the skeletal cube, which may be visually interpreted in two coherent but incompatible ways:

The point of the comparison is this: if someone, through habit or preconception, could only readily interpret the skeletal drawing as a representation of one sort of cube, then the task of helping them to see the other possibility would not have the format of a demonstration. One could not start from some uncontroversial point, and then show that since that was so, some other things followed. For it is not the case that, in the left-hand interpretation, point A is behind point B *because* line CC is behind line DD. Both are true, and inter-entailing; but neither has logical priority. No more can one fully see line CC as behind line DD, before at least in part seeing point A as behind point B.

Demonstration, in the sense of establishing certain points on the basis of other, accepted points, is not really of use in this sort of case.[4] What is needed, rather, is a wholesale change of perspective. Of course, the question of how, if at all, this change may be brought about in a given individual is not a question for logic, but for psychology. In the case of an essay, the question belongs to that branch of psychology called "rhetoric"; and it is my judgment as an amateur student of rhetoric that the method most likely to attain success is simply to present the alternative view, as a whole, at the very beginning of the exercise, in the hope that at least some of my readers will be able to make the shift with only that aid. Thus my second chapter contains almost no argument, and simply puts forward the outline of an interpretation.

---

3. The phenomenon is just a consequence of the fact that any two consistent interpretations of the same set of sentences will be isomorphic.

4. Demonstration's central role comes in establishing that a rival view is untenable because some of its parts have consequences incompatible with other parts. But in this case I am not disputing the consistency of the rival view; I concede that it may be a tenable interpretation. So in attempting to persuade its tenants to switch residence, I must show them that a more attractive view may be had from my premisses.

But of course logic does have some connection to rhetoric; people are generally resistant to believing things that they concurrently believe to be incoherent. And so those who feel that the picture put forward in the first chapter is inconsistent will not accept it as an interpretation of anything. In particular, there is one sort of charge of inconsistency that I must answer if my interpretation is to receive any lasting credence, even among those favorably disposed towards it by the second chapter. Thus the third chapter will be an extended defense of the consistency of the alternative interpretation, against some very skilled and sophisticated attacks launched on it by Myles Burnyeat and Jonathan Barnes.

In the fourth and fifth chapters, I elaborate the details of my interpretation, first in regard to some of the crucial epistemological issues of Sextan skepticism, and then in regard to their ethical consequences. I shall take it that by then the main outlines of the new view have been established, and that its possibility is no longer under scrutiny. Instead, the extended examination will serve the purpose of making its finer points more familiar.

But now I should say a few more words about the sort of isomorphism I mentioned in the beginning, which suggested the cubical analogy. Both interpretations have in common a series of oppositions, between, e.g., belief and lack of belief, disturbance and lack of disturbance, assent and lack of assent, and so on. And both agree about which members of each pair go with which—e.g., both agree that belief, assent and disturbance go together, as do their contrasting privations. Because of this simple binary structure, each interpretation can be depicted by a vertical line, dividing the members of the pairs into two groups. Both interpretations also agree about which side the skeptic belongs on, and which side the professional philosopher belongs on. So much for agreement.

The disagreement between the interpretations involves a third party, peopled by those who are neither avowed skeptics nor avowed members of any other school. These are the ordinary people, or as Sextus refers to them, "those from life". The point at issue is this: on which side of the line ought we to put the ordinary people?

Should we put them among those who have beliefs, or among those who lack them? Among those who assent, and have disturbances, or among those who do not assent and are not disturbed? Should we assimilate them, that is, to the skeptics, or to the pro-

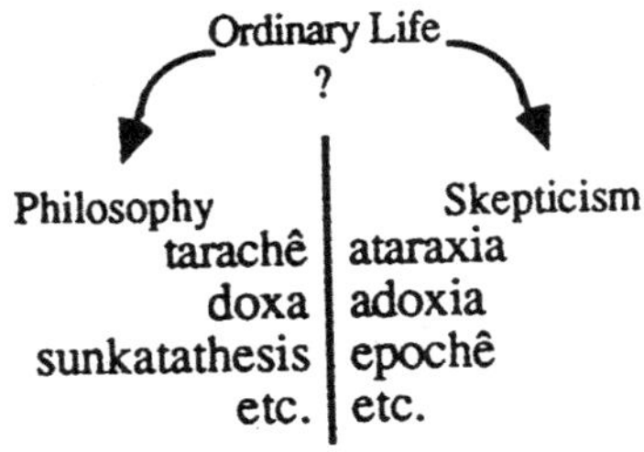

fessional philosophers? (That they must go on one side or the other is a further point of agreement between the two views).

If each of the rival views may be drawn as a pair of columns, divided by a vertical line, then the critical dispute may be envisioned synoptically by considering three columns, with philosophy and skepticism on the flanks, and life in the middle.

The interpretive contest is thus a struggle for life: on which side of Life shall we draw our dividing line? If we follow the traditional interpretation, we shall push the dividing line far to the right of ordinary life, isolating the skeptic. On this view, philosophers are really only one variety of common folk, whose beliefs are at root those of the general gender, although perhaps clarified and systematized. The skeptic, accordingly, is the odd man out; someone engaged in a very peculiar and very unordinary undertaking.

Following the interpretation that I advocate, we should push

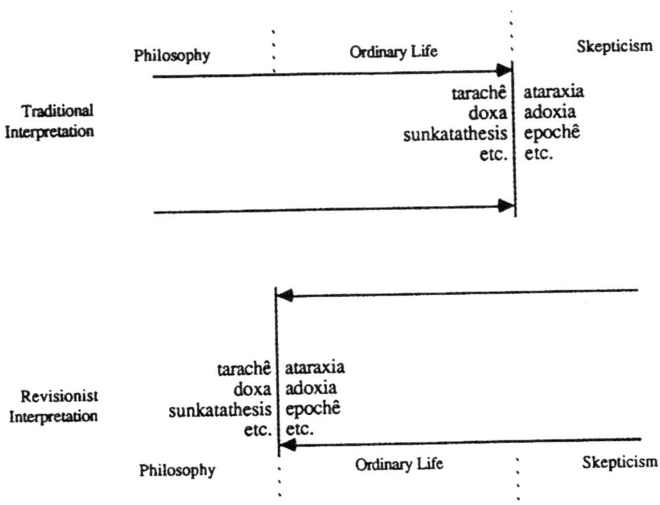

the line to the left, so as to isolate the conscious adherents of selected schools of antiquity. It is they, I shall argue, who are deeply unlike the ordinary person, while the skeptic is the one correctly allied with those from life. Or rather I should say: I shall argue that this is what Sextus means to claim. For that, in the end, is the task that I set for myself: to provide an interpretation of what Sextus Empiricus says about his own brand of skepticism and the life one leads in accordance with it.

Chapter Two

A Positive Presentation of My Interpretation

At the beginning of the dialogue that bears his name, Euthyphro is about to commit the extraordinary act of indicting his own father for murder. Euthyphro says that those who know about it are shocked by his plan, and Socrates himself is shocked. And, one might suspect, Plato has so arranged the case that his readers stand a very good chance of being shocked as well. For the victim of the alleged murder was not anyone of any importance to Euthyphro, a serf in fact, a violent drunkard, and indeed a murderer himself, on Euthyphro's own account. Furthermore, the father's deeds seem quite trivial, and although we must accept Euthyphro's word that they led to the death of the serf, they do not seem to constitute murder. For the father had simply arrested the man for killing a servant while drunk, and then thrown him into a cellar or pit somewhere for safe keeping while he sent to the religious authorities to find out what to do. As it happened, advice was slow in coming, and the serf died of hunger and cold due to the father's inattention. Even if we take Euthyphro's word that his father was callously indifferent to the fate of the prisoner (who would likely have been killed for his crime in any case), we may feel that Euthyphro is being rather precipitous in charging him with murder—and this is apparently the opinion of Euthyphro's contemporaries, including Socrates.

I begin with the *Euthyphro*, because I think it shows us some of the issues that lead the Sextan skeptic to adopt the position he has. In our lives we come to make all manner of decisions and judgments, and the grounds on which we make them, and the manner in which we make them, do not seem at all systematic or precise. Our initial judgments about Euthyphro's rightness in prosecuting his father are affected by a strange miscellany of factors; contingencies of family relation and social class, the moral viciousness of the victim himself, the influence of drugs on his actions, the degree of causal directness or indirectness that links the father's actions to the serf's death, and so on. We pay attention to a number of different considerations, and it may be that, as Euthyphro thinks, some of them are actually irrelevant to the case; and there may be other relevant issues that we overlook. Even when the right questions are asked, they may receive the wrong answer through lack of information or reasoning skill. Our methods seem hopelessly chaotic, and the results are accordingly inconsistent; but nevertheless, we have arrived at certain procedures, which do seem to be handed down from generation to generation, and do produce agreement about many cases; in this case, for instance, most of Euthyphro's contemporaries agree that he is wrong.

Socrates seems to believe that we can do better than this, both in the sense that better procedures are desirable and possible, and in the sense that we ourselves can discover them. By reflecting on our practice, and on our reactions to hypothetical cases, we can come to systematize our methods, and develop our present random practice into an articulate and comprehensive system of rules that would produce the same consistency and agreement about hard cases that we now see in easy ones. The new rules might produce different results from those of the old practice in many cases, but the departures would be shown to be justified, and the old results shown to be unacceptable. Conversely, in those cases where the new system led to the same results, we would now have a much surer foundation than tradition and convention by which to justify them.

The Skeptic, as we find him in Sextus Empiricus' works, seems to be less optimistic about all this. But both Socrates and the Skeptic share an important presupposition: that the judgments made in accordance with the present practice should not be overruled except by a complete, fully worked-out system that is demonstrably capable of eliminating the present anomalies without introducing new ones. Socrates clearly manifests this conservative bias in his insistence that Euthyphro must have some sort of special knowledge about matters of piety and justice in order to prosecute his father. For as he phrases it, the requirement is asymmetrical; he does not say that Euthyphro's present dilemma, or the choice that faces him, requires Euthyphro to have special knowledge. He does not say, as one might be tempted to, that both the option to prosecute and the option not to prosecute are equally in need of justification. He believes from the start that Euthyphro is doing something that is inconsistent with popular beliefs about piety, and it is this fact, that Euthyphro's course of action is unconventional, that obligates him to have some special, more precise knowledge of piety and impiety.

It is in this sense that Socrates' response to the dogmatist is similar to the Sextan skeptic's. Euthyphro is, of course, a dogmatist in the loose sense of having firmly-held convictions and being impatient with disagreement—indeed, he is widely considered one of the duller and more bullish of Socrates' interlocutors. But he is also a dogmatist in the skeptic's more specialized sense. Showing what I mean by this will lead to an examination of most of the crucial issues in the interpretation of Skepticism as it is presented in Sextus Empiricus. For much of what we want to know about the Skeptic has to do with how he differs from the dogmatist, and how he conceives of the dogmatist from whom he so vocally differs.

When I say here that Euthyphro is a dogmatist, and that his dogmatism is particularly illuminating for an understanding of Sextus' skepticism, I have the following points in mind. First of all, he claims to be an expert about theology, and accordingly he claims to know things, some of which are unknown by most people, and all of which are known in a different way. That is, his knowledge of theology is such that where many people believe, e.g., that Zeus is the son of Kronos, he believes this because it is part of his comprehensive theory of the gods, it is supported by other things that he believes, and perhaps because it was acquired in a special way and with a special warrant (notice that he also claims to be an infallible prophet). He also has certain standards of consistency, such that he thinks his present prosecution of his father is consistent with the behavior of Zeus in binding his own father, and such that he takes those who criticize his behavior to be contradicting themselves about the gods' behavior and his own.[1] And in virtue of these standards of consistency, he is willing to draw inferences based on analyses of particular circumstances, analyses that necessarily leave out certain particularities as irrelevant. As part of his overall theory, Euthyphro, has strong beliefs about what sort of considerations are relevant to ethical judgments; it is irrelevant to the justice of a killing whether the victim is a family member or a stranger, and it is irrelevant to the justice of a son's punishment of his father whether they are both gods or humans.

In short, Euthyphro has a big theory. Of course, it is not a theory in the technical sense of being consistent and closed under consequence; that is what Socrates is going to show him. But he has convictions about what the gods are really like, what pious behavior is like, and why it is what it is, convictions that are unconventional and radical, which he uses to generate individual intentions that are unconventional and radical. If he is right about all of this, then a lot of people are wrong; and even where they are right, they may not be right for the reasons that they thought. And Euthyphro is so certain that he is right, that he is willing to ignore conventional opinion, and to trust to his theory for guidance in what is a very important matter, namely the prosecution of his father. He is ready to disregard a variety of factors that we normally do take into consideration when we decide hard cases, and elevate certain other factors to a position that they do not generally have.

By focusing on the radical, even subversive, nature of the dogmatist, we arrive at a different picture of the skeptic. We tend to think of the skeptic as a threat to established beliefs and values, an anarchic destroyer of conventions who leaves nothing unchallenged. But in studying skepticism in Sextus Empiricus, this description actually fits the dogmatist. And it is the skeptic, who,

---

1. It is not at all clear whether the kind of consistency involved here is logical consistency or some substantive principle of ethical universalizability—i.e., whether he is accusing them of a failure of reasoning, or of failing to believe a particular theorem. He might feel that there is a theorem which states (roughly) that whatever is ethical for the gods to do is ethical for humans to do, and a corollary to the effect that whatever may be truly said to be ethical for the gods to do may be truly said to be ethical for humans to do. Then when he accuses others of "saying opposite things about the gods and myself", he might be accusing them of not believing this theorem—i.e., of rejecting a universalizability principle (in the same way in which he thinks one should "say the same things" about the death of a relative and a stranger). But of course this would not be a logical inconsistency. That would only arise if he held that the others actually do believe the theorem and its corollary, and yet fail to conclude from this theorem and from the fact that Zeus' behavior is correct that his doing the same thing is equally correct.

like Socrates, insists that the new and revisionist theory needs justification, and should not be accepted precipitously. Indeed, the skeptic has no standing interest in questioning or examining beliefs at all; I shall argue that this is another great misconception. Modern students tend to think that the skeptic is committed to questioning every belief, and must accordingly make special provisions for any beliefs he has—provisions which generally look viciously inconsistent or at best ad hoc. But in fact the skeptic shows just the same conservative bias that Socrates did. Existing beliefs, those sanctioned by convention and tradition, need no justification at all. Of course they are chaotic and anomalous; they are not obviously rule-governed at present, and may never be amenable to any sort of systematization at all. But one needs no justification to follow them. It is only the dogmatists' theories—theories that claim special insights, perfect universalizability, perfect certitude and sound guidance of action—it is only these challengers that need to show their credentials. And so the skeptic has no general interest in challenging beliefs, unless they are posited as dogmatic beliefs.

It is important to clear up a possible misconception at this point. My claim that in the skeptic's mind traditional and conventional beliefs need no justification must be distinguished from another claim with which it might be confused, namely the claim that in the skeptic's mind these beliefs are justified by their being traditional or conventional. The skeptic does not claim that because a certain belief is traditional, it is thereby justified. It is simply that he does not, in general, examine traditional beliefs. In general, that is; but there is one obvious case in which he will do so. As I have argued, the questioner of traditional beliefs is actually the dogmatist, who promises to revise and systematize the chaos of tradition, even if it means throwing out tub-loads of babies with every drop of bath-water. But it may sometimes happen that, in response to such a dogmatic challenge to tradition, someone undertakes to justify certain beliefs on the basis that they are traditional, or tries to justify all traditional beliefs as a class, or tries to claim that traditional beliefs have a particular epistemological status that makes them self-justifying (e.g., certain conventionalist theories, or the early Greek advocacy of "*nomos*"). But clearly this itself is a dogmatic move, an attempt to give these beliefs a certain absolute status that in general they do not obviously have. Once this is done, a new dogmatism has arisen; and it is only then that the skeptic becomes an investigator of traditions. But the traditions that he investigates are not the ones that he follows; what he attacks are traditions as dogmatic positions. Once they are posited, they become a new challenger to the way we do things, buttressed about with more big theory. And that is not the way in general that we follow traditions and conventions, nor is it how the skeptic follows them. When we learn how to drive a car, the local conventions about, e.g., driving on the right-hand side form part of our education. David Lewis' book on *Conventions* does not. What the skeptic follows is the convention of driving on the right (the American skeptic in America, at any rate); what he attacks are particular accounts of why we do that.

Similar things must be said about sense-perception, as well. The skeptic does not in general question perceptions—his own, or anyone else's. He does not question the perception that he is hot, nor that this is a piece of paper in front of him, nor that the table in front of him is solid, nor that snow is white. None of these require any justification; none of them receive any attack from him, nor are they ever called into question by him. Of course, they are called into question by the dogmatist. The dogmatist routinely constructs theories that undermine and reject any number of apparently obvious things. The dogmatists will not allow us to say that the table in front of us is solid (they will claim it is no different in its essence from a sponge, or a cloud). They will claim to prove that snow is actually black. And faced with these sorts of challenges from dogmatists, it may happen that someone attempts to put our sense-perceptions once and for all on a firmer ground. They may try to devise theories according to which sense-perceptions are always true, or according to which reason is always limited to juggling with the ideas given to it by the senses, or according to which such predicates as "solid" and "white" are held to be learned from such paradigm cases as tables and snow, and accordingly cannot be sensibly denied application in these cases. But once again, these theories are fundamentally dogmatic. And the skeptic, who had no reason to challenge any particular statement that snow is white, will nevertheless be suspicious of theories that attempt to claim that such statements are necessarily true, or are somehow privileged or fundamental. Accordingly, he will investigate these new and improved perceptions, these infallible and foundational perceptions, and try to show that they do not have the properties that the dogmatists of sense-perception claim that they have. He will challenge perceptions exactly to the extent that they are posited dogmatically, by dogmatists.[2] But as with traditions and customs, the perceptions that he himself follows are not the same perceptions that he attacks. What the skeptic follows is the perception that there is a piece of paper in front of him; what he attacks are the infallible perceptions that are the basis of Protagorean or Epicurean epistemology.

My claim, then, is that the skeptic is not the rabid destroyer he is normally seen to be, but rather a conservative and even reactive figure. He has no interest in questioning things generally; he simply feels that individual dogmatists who claim to have developed the correct theory of everything, a theory which can revise and overturn current beliefs at will, must prove their credentials. And so he examines these dogmatic theories, and opposes other dogmatic theories to them. But I should call attention to two striking consequences of my claim: first, that the skeptic can question only what has been posited dogmatically; and second, that in his opposing of argument to argument, he can only use what has already been posited dogmatically. He only attacks dogmatic theories, and he only attacks them with dogmatic theories. Accordingly, as I shall argue, if the partisans of convention had never claimed an elevated status for custom (as, e.g., the foundation of morality) then the skeptic would neither question custom, nor oppose custom to nature. If the partisans of sense-perception had never claimed that all perception is true (and so on), then the skeptic never would have questioned sense-perceptions, nor opposed perceptions to reason. This naturally will have some impact on the perennial question of Sextus' originality; we may not change our assessment, but we may come to wonder whether the question is to the point.

The question of whether the skeptic can live his skepticism becomes relatively straightforward now, and the answer that the skeptic should give is plain. If faced with this question, the skeptic should respond that he lives exactly as everyone else does—all of

2. Again, this is a preview of my argument against Barnes' claim (in Barnes 1983) that the skeptic cannot even use everyday judgments, because after the skeptic destroys proofs of "*adêla*" he also destroys "*enargeia*", or evidence. What Barnes fails to respect is that the "evidence" that the skeptic attacks is the self-evident, foundational perceptions of certain broadly empiricist epistemological theories. It is only because "*enargeia*" was posited as a criterion that the skeptic attacks it; and he only attacks its use *as a* criterion.

the non-fanatics, that is—and that although it has its drawbacks nothing better has come along. The skeptic believes exactly what everyone else believes, and in exactly the same ways; his beliefs are not somehow of a different nature from anyone else's. And there is no obvious or readily specifiable limit to the beliefs that he can have, either; the only way of spelling out what beliefs he will not have is to say that he does not assent to any of the dogmatists' theories (or to their contradictories). And this, once again, is not a matter of content so much as a matter of attitude towards the content; the dogmatists posit their beliefs, and thereby claim for them certain properties of certitude, explanatory power, and so on. The skeptic just believes things, in the way most people do. And he believes exactly what most people do; whatever he believed before becoming a skeptic, whatever he grew up believing, whatever people in general believe, all of these things are available to him.

But, once again, the description of that list is not the same as a justification of its contents. That is, the skeptic believes what most people believe, and in one sense it is probably accurate to say that he believes it because most people believe it. But of course that is not the justification for his believing it. 1, for instance, believe that the earth goes around the sun. And in one sense, it is probably accurate to say that I believe it just because most people around me believe it, and because I grew up believing it and being told that it was so. But I certainly do not feel that my belief is *justified* by the fact that most people believe it, and in that sense it is wholly false to say that I believe it because most people believe it—my belief is not justified, nor do I hold it to be justified, by that fact. But why should my belief be justified at all? Who wants me to justify it? Not, I claim, the skeptic; rather it is the dogmatist who is always asking us to change our minds, always promising better, truer, more certain beliefs. Accordingly, it is the dogmatists who must present evidence that their new beliefs really are better, really do avoid the anomalies that—as the skeptic readily admits—are a part of the present state.

So I take it that the skeptic has a wide range of beliefs, and that these beliefs are not somehow of a funny or special type. And I take it that the skeptic, like all of his contemporaries (except those unseasonable Pre-Socratics, the Epicureans)[3], can claim with some

3. I suspect that this is what Timon means by calling Epicurus the "last of the Physicists" (fr. 825.1).

justification that he is fundamentally a follower of Socrates. He too is looking for some better way, some way of transcending the anomaly in things that caused him to begin his search for truth. And he too finds himself surrounded by dogmatists, all of them convinced that they already have answers that surpass those of the common herd. And he too sets to work to see if these putative systems really do have the consistency, certainty, and truth that they each claim. His field of enquiry is restricted to whatever views are posited by the dogmatists; the burden of proof is on those who would innovate. The beliefs of the majority, and his own beliefs, go unchallenged.

The interpretation of Sextus argued for in this thesis has two further revisionary consequences, which are in disagreement with the received wisdom about ancient skepticism. Both involve alleged points of difference between ancient and modern skepticism; one involving the practical consequences of skepticism, and the other its target. If one turns to any standard work on Greek philosophy, one may find it said that the ancient skeptic somehow followed out the practical consequences of skepticism more seriously than does the modern skeptic; and that the ancient skeptic challenged all beliefs, where the modern skeptic challenges only knowledge. Each of these distinctions seems to me more wrong than right.

The greater seriousness of the ancient skeptic is a theme often adverted to by historians of ancient skepticism; most frequently, it seems, when they wish to twit their modern colleagues for lacking historical perspective. Annas and Barnes put the contrast this way: "'Philosophical' doubt [i.e., the doubt of the modern skeptic] is thus essentially idle: it cannot, by definition, have any bearing on action. It is easy to think that it is also a sham....[T]he ancient sceptics had no interest in philosophical doubt. The doubt they expected to induce was ordinary, non-philosophical doubt; it excluded beliefs, and it was therefore a practical doubt .... " [4] They then commend at several points the "greater interest and seriousness of the ancient variety"[5], and call ancient skepticism "more compelling and more significant philosophically".[6]

Unfortunately, such glowing assessments of the ancients'

4. Annas and Barnes 1985 p.9.
5. Annas and Barnes 1985 p.9.
6. Annas and Barnes 1985 p. 171

greater earnest and resolve are purchased at the cost of correspondingly low assessments of their sanity, perspicacity, and honesty. They were doing something far more noble and *engagé* than we in our commons rooms ever do; poor dears, they must have been quite mad![7] Or: what a shame they failed to see the undertaking is shot through with inconsistencies; or saw it and lived behind a mask of deceit! All of these negative characterizations are the constant companions of thinking that the practical consequences of ancient skepticism would have been vast and drastic. In fact, I shall argue that the Sextan skeptic, just like the modern one, will not be reduced to shrugging if asked whether a kettle of water on the stove will boil.

Indeed, to state my position as strongly as possible, I claim that most modern historians of ancient philosophy—myself and my readers thus among them—are themselves Sextan skeptics. This statement is liable to misunderstanding, because it seems to report an extraordinary finding about the academic community. It seems to involve the application of a familiar predicate, "Sextan skeptic", to a familiar subject, "historians of philosophy", in such a way as to attribute strange, new and unsuspected properties to our colleagues. Accordingly, the statement seems to require us to revise our beliefs about our colleagues. This is not what I intend. Rather, I want my auditors to hold fixed the beliefs they have about their colleagues, and instead revise their beliefs about the import of the term "Sextan Skeptic".

Now, the usual way of structuring a sentence so as to explain an unfamiliar A in terms of a familiar B is to say something on the lines of "A's are B's", or perhaps "A's are just like B's"; the familiar predicate explains the unfamiliar subject. To an audience familiar with chicken, but unfamiliar with rattlesnake, one says "the taste of rattlesnake is (the same as) the taste of chicken" or "rattlesnake is (tastes) just like chicken".

On this model, the most straightforward way for me to explain my views of Sextan skepticism in terms of more familiar things is to say "the beliefs of the Sextan skeptic are the beliefs of anyone else" or "Sextan skeptics are just like anyone else". But unfortunately, there is a tradition of supposing that the kind of resemblance involved is only a superficial mimicry; that they may

7. Annas and Barnes 1985 p. 171 allege "depression and neuroses" as probable consequences of living skeptically ; Burnyeat 1980a p.41 says that the skeptic's life will be a "hollow shell".

be just like other people in some surface way, but still are not really like other people. So I cannot use this method of making my meaning unambiguous.

Further underlining of adverbs seems unlikely to bring greater clarity. Instead, I take advantage of a feature of the identity relation, namely that it is symmetrical.[8] If skeptics were clever mimics of ordinary folk, it would not follow that ordinary folk were clever mimics of skeptics; "clever mimic of" is not a symmetrical relation. But if skeptics just *are* (some) ordinary folk, then (some) ordinary folk just are skeptics. Which ordinary folk? Well, the ones who are distinguished from their fellows by their interest in, say, the details of Plato's cosmology in the *Timaeus*—i.e. historians of ancient philosophy. Not the ones who actually believe in fire-triangles; those, according to Sextus, are dogmatists and so disjoint from ordinary folk. But I take it that most historians do not subscribe to the tenets of the schools they study, and instead believe roughly what those around them believe. That is how I think we should understand Sextus as well. And the most vivid way to express the literalness of my claim that Sextan skeptics are ordinary people (antiquarian curiosity aside), is by reversing it: ordinary people are Sextan skeptics.

As well as seeming implausible, this conclusion may seem disappointing to those who hope to find in the study of history some thing more than a reflection of their own surroundings. It may even seem a very grave sin on my part against the spirit of historically sensitive reconstruction, that I should assimilate ancient ways of thought to our own. But this charge, it seems to me, should instead be laid against those who overlook the deep strangeness of the dogmatical schools of antiquity, particularly those with which Sextus was most familiar, namely the Epicureans and Stoics. Part of the difficulty in understanding Sextus comes from a failure to understand how odd these dogmatists were, which in turn encourages the mistaken view that ordinary people would come out as dogmatists on Sextus' classification.

8. I thank John Konkle for showing me that this was another way of stating my position.

CHAPTER THREE

A Defense of the Possibility of the Revisionist Interpretation[1]

INTRODUCTION

In the last chapter I presented an outline of the interpretation that I favor, postponing its elaboration for the third and fourth chapters, and its detailed defense for the present chapter. So I now turn to a consideration of the other interpretations usually placed upon the writings of Sextus Empiricus, and the criticisms that their proponents have made of the suggestion that the skeptic can have anything like ordinary beliefs.

According to the traditional interpretation, the Sextan Skeptic is engaged in an extreme and exotic epistemological project,

1. In place of the original third chapter of my thesis, I here print a version improved through its appearance in two previous published incarnations. The replacement covers all of the material to be found in the third chapter of the original dissertation, clarified and in some places augmented, and omits only some mistakes and unclarities. This material first appeared in Brennan 1994. At that time I took the opportunity to express my gratitude to Michael Frede, Myles Burnyeat, Richard Sorabji, M. M. McCabe, David Furley, and John Cooper; my gratitude to them has only grown in the intervening years. In 1997, Juha Sihvola, acting as the editor of the *Acta Philosophica Fennica*, asked my permission to reprint Brennan 1994 in a special number he was planning on skepticism"; this will appear as Brennan 2000.". I thank him for his efforts to make the piece better known, and for the impetus he gave me to revise the 1994 version, in particular adding the "Postscript 1999" which is included here. And as always, my deepest thanks go to Liz Karns.

opposed to both the ordinary person and the non-skeptical philosopher. A universal critic, he attacks all of our beliefs, both sacred and profane; he not only challenges belief in God and morality, he also challenges belief in the existence of anything outside his own sensorium—perhaps even the existence of his opponents. Because of his skeptical arguments, the Skeptic has come to the conclusion that all beliefs are unjustified, and so has concluded that he should not have any beliefs, and to the best of his ability does not have any beliefs.[2]

There may well have been, or even be, people who advocate skepticism of this kind. For the sake of convenience, I shall call this kind of skepticism "rabid skepticism". Like hydrophobic dogs, rabid skeptics roam about savaging everything in their way, even biting themselves, and usually die of their own heedlessness, falling over cliffs or being run over by cars. And like other mad dogs, they are often found in the company of Englishmen, or rather Britons; to say that it is traditional to view the Skeptic this way, is to include in the tradition such disparate figures as David Hume and Samuel Johnson,[3] but to exclude such figures as Montaigne and some other continental writers.

This British tradition has tended to take Sextus Empiricus as the paradigm of a rabid Skeptic, and the rabid interpretation of Sextus is currently being championed with great skill and learning by Myles Burnyeat, Jonathan Barnes, and other of their compatriots. Between proponents of this view there may be disagreement about whether universal doubt is the Skeptic's intended goal, or only the unintended, perhaps even unnoticed, consequence of his attacks on belief. But both variations of this view agree that, if put into practice consistently and conscientiously, the Skeptical system presented in Sextus' writings would require its adherent to live without any beliefs beyond those justified by being unassailable, as for instance his beliefs about whether or not he is feeling a pain

---

2. These steps are usefully distinguished and discussed by Fogelin 1983.
3. Johnson's view of the consequences of Pyrrhonism may be seen in ll. 343-6 of his translation of Juvenal X, "On the Vanity of Human Wishes":

> Where then shall Hope and Fear their objects find?
> Must dull Suspense [i.e. *epokhê*] corrupt the stagnant mind?
> Must helpless man, in ignorance sedate,
> Roll darkling down the torrent of his fate?

These lines, which reflect the common 18th-century British view of Skepticism, may owe something to Hume's Treatise, published ten years earlier, but correspond to nothing in Juvenal.

right now. Naturally, this sort of Skeptic is vulnerable to the charge that adopting his stance makes life unlivable, or at best reduces one's life to some sub-human, vegetative state. Both Barnes, in his article "The Beliefs of a Pyrrhonist",[4] and Burnyeat, in his article "Can the Skeptic live his Skepticism?",[5] portray Sextus as this sort of Skeptic, and tax him with different varieties of the traditional *argumentum ad phyton*.[6] For it seems that a life lived with only beliefs of this sort would be very different from ordinary life; so that when Sextus sometimes talks as though he does lead an ordinary life, this view concludes that he can only be referring to the superficies of observable behavior. A life so different from our own on the inside, seems only more horrible if it mirrors our lives on the outside; a kind of masquerade or mimicry, but a mimicry of oneself, a sort of holding of oneself at arm's length.

An alternative to this picture is supported by those students who do not find in Sextus the advocation of universal doubt, but only of a more focused and limited doubt. For Sextus says on many occasions that the Skeptic examines not all beliefs, but only "*dogmata*". And by "*dogmata*" Sextus means the principles and tenets characteristic of the professional schools of philosophy, as for instance the Epicurean's belief in invisible atoms, or Platonist's belief in eternal, unchanging forms.[7] Now if it is only beliefs of this sort that he attacks, then it seems that his stock of permissible beliefs has just increased immensely. For the Skeptic can now believe, not only that he is feeling a pain, but that the pain is in his foot, and that it is caused by his shoes; and he can believe that there is a more comfortable pair in the room next door. Indeed, it seems that there is now nothing to prevent his acting on these beliefs, and changing his shoes. For none of these beliefs, or the actions that involve them, appear to require him to believe in Epicurean atoms, Platonic forms, or things of that sort; and so his failure to have beliefs about things of that sort does not seem to require such a drastic change in his life, either externally or internally.

The second component of the revisionist view is the observation that the arguments against *dogmata* quite generally employ

4. Barnes 1983, pp. 5-43.
5. Burnyeat 1980a.
6. See AM XI.163.
7. This point was maintained by Sedley 1983 (fn. 67, p.28), further supported by Barnes 1983 (pp. 15-22), and finally conceded by Burnyeat in Burnyeat 1984 (fn. 13, p.229).

premisses that are only binding on someone who is already committed to one of the Dogmatic schools. Sextus will begin, for instance, with a particular school's conception of what motion is, and then show that, according to that conception, motion is impossible. By arguing in this way, his arguments are successful *ad hominem* in showing the Dogmatical philosophers that there are inconsistencies within their systems; but there is no reason why they should have any effect on someone who does not already subscribe to a Dogmatical school. So the revisionist picture assumes that the Skeptic's arguments are propounded dialectically, in terms to which the Skeptic's opponents are committed.

Finally, the revisionist interpretation takes the Sextan Skeptic's claims to live an ordinary life as sincere and accurate, neither disingenuous nor self-deceived. If he says that he lives according to the ordinary and common way of life, the revisionist view does not take this to indicate merely superficial imitation and external conformity, guided by a complex and radically unordinary inner motivation. That would not be living *as* we do, but rather living *as if* he lived as we do. But the Skeptic has no reasons not to believe what everyone else ordinarily does, and so there is no reason to attribute such a strange project to him.

The revisionist interpretation is the one that, on balance, seems to me most plausible. Those who see Sextus as a rabid Skeptic have a variety of arguments against it. I want to examine two of them today, each of which denies that the Skeptic can have ordinary beliefs, and show why I do not think that they decisively rule out the revisionist view. Even if I succeed in this demonstration,[8] I shall have done little to resolve the *diaphônia* within the field; but I hope that the attempt will be of value in any case.

PART I: CRITERIA

Jonathan Barnes' position is like the one alluded to above, according to which universal doubt is not the Skeptic's intended goal, but rather the unintended consequence of other goals. For Barnes notices many of the passages throughout the Outlines of Pyrrhonism (PH) that support the revisionist view of Sextan skepticism, but concludes only that there are two strains of skepticism in

8. "*Dei memnêsthai anthrôpon onta*," as Aristotle says in his *Peri T'agathou* (fr.27), "*ou monon ton eutuchounta, alla kai ton apodeiknunta*."

Sextus, a traditionally rabid one, which he describes as "rustic" (following a comment of Galen's) and a strain closer to the revisionist view I am advocating, which he calls "urbane". He admits a number of points in favor of the urbane interpretation, whereby the Sextan Skeptic is an advocate of ordinary beliefs and ordinary life who rejects only the technical doctrines of the philosophical schools. But he argues that this urbane stance collapses into rusticity, if its consequences are followed out. In particular, Barnes studies Sextus' discussions of logic and the criterion, and concludes from them that "the PH Pyrrhonist emerges as a rustic." Here is his argument.[9]

> 1) If the PH Pyrrhonist can have any ordinary beliefs, then he can have the belief, for instance, that the bath-water is tepid. (This taken by a sort of universal instantiation).
>
> 2) If the PHP can have the belief that the bath-water is tepid, then he must have a criterion of truth. ("A Pyrrhonist will only believe that the water is tepid if he judges it to be so; and he can only judge it to be so if he possesses a criterion of truth by which to judge it.")
>
> 3) If he has a criterion of truth, then he has a *dogma*, i.e. a scientifico-philosophical theory.
>
> 4) If he has a *dogma*, i.e. a scientifico-philosophical theory, then he is not any sort of Skeptic, not even an urbane Skeptic.
>
> 5) But it is agreed on all sides that he is some sort of Skeptic, at least an urbane Skeptic.
>
> 6) Accordingly, by 5&4, he does not have a *dogma*.
>
> 7) Accordingly, by 6&3, he does not have a criterion of truth.
>
> 8) Accordingly, by 7&2, he cannot have the belief that the bath-water is tepid.
>
> 9) Accordingly, by 8&1, he cannot have any ordinary beliefs at all.

9. I have regimented Barnes' argumentation here to some extent, but he made no objection to its general fidelity in a letter written to the editor of BICS refereeing the article.

So the assumption that Sextus is an urbane Skeptic leads to the conclusion that he is a rustic Skeptic: "In rejecting *dogmata* he explicitly rejects any scientifico-philosophical theory; but he implicitly rejects all other beliefs as well."[10]

I believe that this argument has a number of problems. Barnes himself anticipates objections to what I have labeled premiss 3) above. "...[I]t might be objected that, although in order to judge that p I must possess a criterion, it is not true that in order to judge that p I must believe that I possess a criterion." It is the belief that one has a criterion that constitutes a *dogma*; mere possession is not illegal. So perhaps the Skeptic could possess one, unwittingly, and use it to form judgements, without thereby having a scientifico-philosophical *dogma*. "But," replies Barnes, "could a Pyrrhonist judge that p after *reflecting* on the existence of a criterion and reaching *epochê* on the matter?"[11] His thought seems to be that after the Skeptic has considered Epicurean arguments for their criterion and against other criteria, and Stoic arguments for their criterion and against other criteria, and has at last come to think that none of them have any persuasive or dissuasive force at all, he will suspend judgement about the existence of a criterion. But why should this stop the Skeptic from judging that p? It may well stop the Dogmatists from judging that p, but why should it have any bearing on the Skeptic's actions at all? The Dogmatists think that judging is a very serious affair; some of them think that assent to a falsehood is just as great a sin as eating one's children or maliciously knocking over trash-cans. And they believe that a particular sort of criterion must be available before one judges; consequently, if they come to believe that it is not available, they must abandon all judgement. But the Skeptic has no reason to subscribe to either of these beliefs. He has no reason to think that one needs a criterion before one judges; that is just a peculiar consequence of the Dogmatists' theories about action and psychology.

So it seems that the Skeptic has no obligation to agree that a criterion is required for beliefs, and in fact has good reason to doubt it. For it seems to be a consequence of the very epistemological theories that make this claim, that they render their adherents incapable of having any beliefs at all. This is what the Skeptic's argument is designed to demonstrate to, e.g., the Stoic. The

10. Barnes 1983 p. 28.

11. Barnes 1983 fn. 76, p. 28 ; emphasis in the original.

Dogmatists are forced by their own tenets to suspend judgement, not simply because the Skeptic shows them that they do not have a criterion, but precisely because it is one of their tenets that one should judge only if one has a criterion. This second tenet is one of the *dogmata* that leads to the Dogmatists' overthrow; why should the Skeptic believe it himself?

It is unclear, then, why we should grant Barnes premiss 2):—and more to the point, it is unclear why Sextus should. Urbane skepticism collapses into rustic, only if ordinary beliefs require scientific criteria. Yet certainly this itself is a prime piece of *dogma*, the claim that if one can believe that the bath-water is tepid, then one must have a criterion of belief. Sextus, it seems to me, would be perfectly justified in rejecting it outright.

As it turns out, however, what Sextus does is rather more interesting. At several places in his writings (PH I.21-22, PH II.14-15, and AM VII. 29-33), Sextus offers an account of different senses of the word "*kritêrion*".[12] First, "*kritêrion*" is said both of criteria for action or life, and of criteria for *katalêpsis* or infallible cognition. Then the first group, which is also referred to as the "normal rules or observation of life" (*biôtikê têrêsis*) is divided into four sub-groups: natural sensation and thought; affections like hunger and thirst; customs and traditions; and the precepts of crafts. The second group, containing the criteria of *katalêpsis* or infallible cognition, is divided into three sub-groups, containing the general, special, and most special criteria. Into the category of general criteria go all kinds of criteria of *katalêpsis*, "even the natural ones, such as sight." The special criteria include "every technical standard of *katalêpsis*, such as the rule and the compass." The most special criteria include "every technical standard of *katalêpsis* of a non-evident object; but according to this sense the ordinary standards (*ta biôtika kritêria*) are not regarded as criteria, only logical criteria and those which the Dogmatists employ for judging the truth." The resulting classification looks like the figure below.

If we consider these seven categories—four for the criteria of life, three for the criteria of infallible cognition—we may be struck by the impression that they are not properly exclusive. That is, it seems that sense-perception, as for instance sight, occurs both among the criteria for action (the first sub-group of the four) and among the criteria for *katalêpsis* (the first sub-group of the three). Such craft-implements as yard-sticks and compasses also seem to

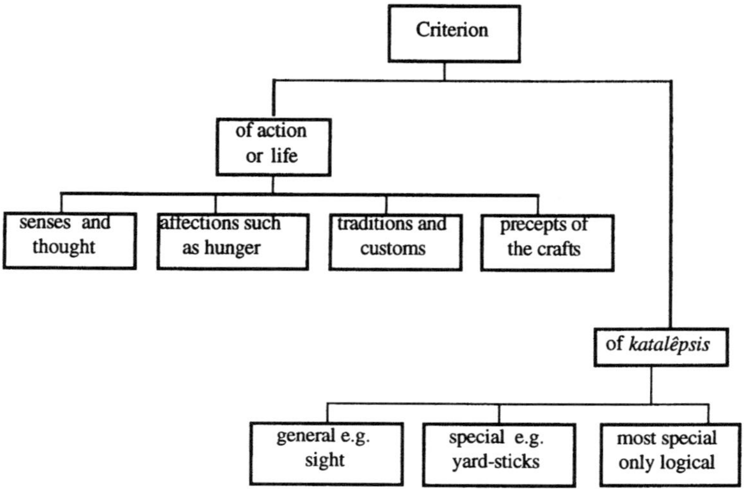

belong just as much to the fourth sub-group of the first group, i.e. the precepts of the crafts, as to the second sub-group of the second group.

The suspicion that the first two criteria of *katalêpsis* cannot be distinguished from the criteria of life or action is further strengthened by the qualification appended to the description of the most special criteria of *katalêpsis*, that "according to this sense, the criteria of life (*ta biôtika kritêria*) are no longer included." For it seems fairly certain that the three senses of "criterion" in the sense of a criterion of infallible cognition are being presented to us in order of increasing exclusivity (general, special, most special), so that the bottom right corner of the diagram above should be modified as seen below.

Now if the criteria of life are excluded from all three criteria of *katalêpsis*, it is very misleading only to mention this at the last stage, viz. the most special. On the other hand, if the criteria of life really are only excluded at the last stage, then they presumably are included into the first two stages, viz. the general and special senses. And if this is so, if items like sight and hearing and rulers and compasses show up both among the criteria of life or action and among the criteria of infallible cognition, then how are we to

12. Heintz 1932 compares the pseudo-Galenic *History of Philosophy*, which offers a three-fold distinction of senses of "*hairesis*" (p.603 in Diels Doxographi), and a distinction of senses of "*kritêrion*" (Diels p. 606) quite close to that in Sextus.

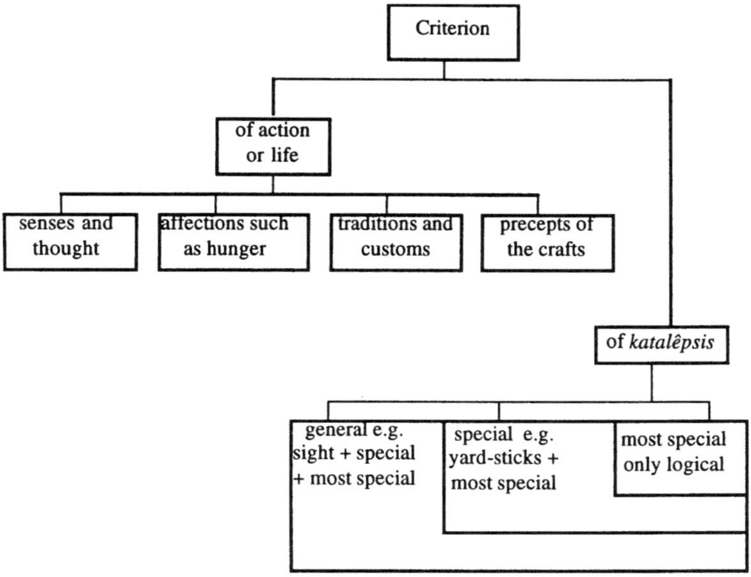

understand that initial dichotomy?

The answer, I propose, is simply that Sextus is not always careful—for reasons that will become apparent—to remind us that these are not different kinds of criteria, but different senses of the word "criterion". There is no reason why an item like sight should not appear in several places; it is simply being treated differently at each mention, having one or another sense of the word "criterion" applied to it. As a criterion of action or life, sight is just one of the things we use in order to get about, avoid precipices, and live our normal lives. As a criterion of *katalêpsis*, it is something far more; it is the infallible perception of the Epicureans on which they base the existence of atoms, or the source of the Stoics' cognitive impressions which form the starting-points for the Sage's syllogisms. Sight per se, or the carpenter's or surveyor's use of the yard-stick, are never the target of Sextus' attacks; it is only when the Dogmatists try to erect their systems on these foundations that the Skeptic challenges them. This is exactly what Sextus says he will do, both at PH II and at AM VII. In the first passage, he introduces the criteria of *katalêpsis* by saying "The criterion with which our argument is concerned (*peri hou ho logos estin*) has three senses: general, special and most special..." And having described the most special, he then says "We propose, therefore, in the first place to discuss the logical criterion [i.e. the most special]." So his treatment of the criterion begins with the most special, but we know from the start that he will examine all three parts of the criterion of *katalêpsis*. And since the first two senses (the general and the special) are also applied to items such as sight and yard-sticks that are sometimes used as criteria of life or action, we should not be surprised if Sextus later examines the claims of certain Dogmatists to have found criteria of truth or infallible cognition in these same items.

This is also the procedure that Sextus describes less carefully when at AM VII. 34 he says, "we propose to examine in the first place the logical criterion, which the philosophers harp on, and subsequently each of the criteria of ordinary life (*peri hekastou tôn kata ton bion*)."This is a less careful way of referring to the general and special criteria of infallible cognition, because it gives the false impression that he plans to examine the criteria of action and life. But this certainly cannot be right, since he starts each of the treatments of the criterion by specifying that he is only investigating criteria of *katalêpsis*, not criteria of action and life. And it is easy enough to see where the confusion arises from; for sight, e.g., is used both as a criterion of life (by everyone) and as a criterion of *katalêpsis* (by certain Dogmatists), whereas the logical criteria (= the most special) are used only by Dogmatists. So when Sextus has in mind the contrast between the most specialized "criterion of *katalêpsis*" , i.e. the logical criterion, and the other two groups (the general and more special), the most salient difference is that the latter include items (such as sight and yard-sticks) which are also described as criteria of life. That is why he refers to the eventual discussion of sight as a criterion of infallible cognition by saying, misleadingly, that he will later examine the criteria of life. It is true that he will examine sight, and it is true that this is, among other things, a criterion of life. But among other things, it is also a criterion of *katalêpsis*, and it is exactly as a criterion of *katalêpsis* that he will examine it, not as a criterion of life. The same looseness is in play when he refers to the criteria of *katalêpsis* that are not so-called in the most special sense as "*ta biôtika*".

It is crucial to an understanding of these passages to note that these different senses of the term "criterion" do not directly pick out items like sight or yard-sticks. Sight is not a criterion in any of the individual senses of "criterion" identified by Sextus here. Sight considered in a certain way is a criterion of a certain kind. Considered as a guide for normal life, it is a criterion of action or life. Considered as an infallible foundation for the correct theory of everything, it is a criterion of *katalêpsis*. But if we simply ask what kind of criterion sight is—just sight—there is no obvious answer. We might say it appears in the schema twice, or we might say that it does not appear at all; I do not immediately see what will turn on the decision. But much turns on understanding the distinction that Sextus proposes, and the nature of the distinction. For it undermines Barnes' argument that the Skeptic must have a dogmatic criterion, as well as his charge that Sextus sometimes attacks the uses of normal life.

With the distinction between senses of the word "criterion" in mind, we can now see that premisses 2) and 3) contain an ambiguity that Barnes misses, despite the fact that Sextus thought it was so central he put it in the first few pages of his Outlines. Premiss 2) says "In order to have an ordinary belief, one must have a criterion"; yes, this might be roughly right on some very attenuated notion of criterion, e.g. the sort of criterion of action that Sextus professes having. Premiss 3) says "But if one has a criterion, then one has a scientifico-philosophical belief, i.e. a dogma". Yes, this too might be right, but only if one means exactly the other kind of criterion, that is, an infallible foundational criterion of truth. That kind is certainly dogmatic. And that kind is specifically cited by Sextus as the object of his enquiries and doubts. But that kind is also quite superfluous for arriving at some belief about the temperature of the water. The way that we come to believe that the water is tepid is by, e.g., dipping a finger into it, or, if we are practicing the confectioner's craft, by dipping a thermometer into it. In a sense we have used a criterion in order to form our belief; we employed some means of judging the water's temperature. It would be otherwise if we had flipped a coin and then announced the water was tepid or frigid as the coin landed heads or tails. In some fairly straightforward way, that would fail to be a case of judging that the water is tepid. To that extent, the finger or the thermometer is a criterion; it is the reason why we do this and not that, as Sextus says of the criterion of life. But it is certainly not a criterion of infallible cognition; we are all aware of how we can be led astray by such methods. Sextus is pointing out here that the normal person's use of a finger or thermometer is not bound up with any claim to infallibility or deeper insight; the normal person is not a Dogmatist. When we normally judge that the water is tepid, we are not, on the one hand, claiming perfect infallibility, or claiming that no further evidence or deliberation could cause us to change our mind about this affirmation. That may be what a Stoic Sage does in affirming something, but it is certainly not what we do on the hundreds of occasions each day when we affirm or believe something. But on the other hand, we are also not adopting any sort of exotic epistemological stance, to the effect that our affirmation stops at our finger-tips, or perhaps at our sensorium, and according to which we affirm that we are having tepid sense-data but take no position about the temperature of the water, or its existence, or even our own existence an instant before or hence. Neither of these is obviously what we do when we believe or affirm that the water is tepid. We just see how it feels, and if it appears tepid then we do one thing, or if it appears hot perhaps we do a different thing. That is just what Sextus claims the Skeptic does; he follows how things feel, and lives and acts accordingly.

So the argument that ordinary beliefs require criteria which require *dogmata* flies directly in the face of Sextus' express intentions and distinctions. So does the argument that because Sextus sometimes attacks normal life, he cannot be sincerely advocating it. For the passages that appear to contain attacks on normal life are merely further reflections of the fact that some of the items which are used by everyone as criteria of normal life are also sometimes put forward by the Dogmatists as criteria of infallible cognition. This is clearly the case with the various attacks on sense-perception, and I believe it is also the case with the attack on the *consensus omnium* argument for the existence of gods (e.g. at AM IX.61 et seq.). Sextus says that one of his criteria for action and life is the tradition of customs and laws. And in some sense it seems to be right to say that the reason why we go to church on Sunday rather than Tuesday and worship this way rather than that is precisely because that is how everyone around us does it and has done it. To that extent, universal agreement about the existence of gods is a criterion, in the sense of a reason for doing this rather than that. But it is not a criterion of truth in the sense of an infallible guide to a deeper reality, as certain Dogmatists would like to say. It is the Dogmatists (in this case the Stoics) who in response to other dogmatic denials of gods, elevate ordinary opinion to a criterial status that it does not obviously have. For, among other things, surely most of those peoples who believe in gods do not justify their belief, as the Stoics do, via the *consensus omnium*!

Similar remarks apply to a passage in which Sextus appears to be attacking common linguistic usage, or *sunêtheia*. All through AM I, Sextus advocates adherence to *sunêtheia* as a guide to speaking and writing, and it seems fairly clear how linguistic usage fits into the fourfold criterion of living normally and undogmatically. For instance, instead of adhering to an elaborate system of rules for speaking correct Greek, derived from technical linguistic theory, he will simply aim to be understood by those around him, using the words most suited to his auditors (AM I.234).[13] Thus when we see him attack *sunêtheia* at AM VIII.128-129, we may at first think that the traditional reading is gaining some support for its picture of the Skeptic as a loose cannon firing on its own position:

> For we must allow ordinary speech to make use of inexact terms, as it does not seek after what is true as regards the nature of things (*to pros tên phusin alêthes*), but what is supposed to be true (*to pros tên doxan*). Thus we say that we are digging a well and weaving a cloak and building a house, but not with exactness; for if there is a well, it is not being dug but it has been dug; and if there is a cloak, it is not being woven but it has been woven. So that in ordinary life and common conversation inexact speech is in place, but when we are inquiring into things as regards their nature (*ta pros tên phusin*), then we must stick to accuracy (*akribeias*). AM VIII.129

When one first reads this passage it may seem like a dangerous statement for Sextus to make. For after all, does he not himself engage in *katachrêsis* —inexact speech—at times?[14] Is his Skeptical way not grounded on the observance of customary usage? How can he now turn and attack this very foundation? Surely this seems like the sort of rustic move that Barnes detects in the earlier passages.

But in this case, as in the ones that Barnes mentions, there is a perfectly sensible reason why Sextus should attack *ho bios*; once again, it is being incorporated into a dogmatic position. In the larger context of the argument, we can see that certain Stoics have claimed that tf conjunctions (i.e. conjunctions with at least one false conjunct as well as true conjuncts) are false, regardless of the presence of true conjuncts. And others have argued that a conjunction with both true and false conjuncts is no more false than true. And someone could even claim that a conjunction with several true conjuncts and one false conjunct is true—and this, after all, would be no more an act of bare assertion than the Stoics' claim that it is false, if that is not supported by arguments.

It is in response to this move that the Stoics try to find support in ordinary language. They support their analysis of the tf conjunction by appealing to our normal habit of saying that a cloak, for instance, is torn when any part of it is torn, even if large expanses of it are still whole:

> But, [the Stoics] say, just as in ordinary life (*hôsper en tôi biôi*) we do not say that the garment which is in most parts sound, but in a small part torn, is sound because of its more numerous and sound parts, but we call it torn because of its small part which is torn, so also with the conjunction,—even if it has only one part false and several true, the whole will be called false after the one part. AM VIII.128

If in normal life someone were to say that a cloak was torn when it only had one rip in one area, then there is no reason to think that Sextus would criticize that usage. What he does criticize is the attempt to found an extensive and Dogmatical system of logic (part of what is at stake here is the Stoic fifth indemonstrable) on top of normal usage, when normal usage does not seem to support it. Normal usage does not support it because, as Sextus is quick to point out, sometimes we say that the mixed item is no more black than white; which parallel should we follow?

Normal usage does not obviously support one rendering of the tf conjunction any more than it supports another; the Stoic attempt to turn it into a support is typically Dogmatical. And Sextus has a particularly full license to twit the Stoics about an appeal to ordinary language; for this school above all had a reputation for loving recherché and technical terms, and for inventing neologisms to suit (or disguise) the needs of their doctrines. Just as in the other

13. He offers as an example of this lexical flexibility two different words for "chamber-pot", the more elevated "*stamnion*", and the more colloquial "*amidion*". This second word is very rare, being found only here and in a fragment of the "Telauges" of Aeschines of Sphettos (fr. 43 Dittmar), quoted by Dio Chrysostom (or. LV.22). It is striking that Dio's aim in quoting the dialogue is to laud Socrates (as portrayed in this case by Aeschines) for his ability to make his diction and illustrations appropriate to the characters with whom he is speaking.

cases, then, this quotation gives us no reason to think that the Skeptic has a general interest in questioning the normal conduct of life. It is only when the Dogmatists attempt to enlist *ho bios* into their schemes that Sextus crafts arguments that seem to call *ho bios* into question. And even in these cases, what they call into question is not *ho bios* itself, but the particular role assigned to it by the Dogmatists in question.

Far from attacking the conduct of life to which he claims allegiance, Sextus only opposes beliefs that have been posited dogmatically; furthermore, in his opposing of argument to argument, he only enlists in the opposition other things that have been posited dogmatically. He only attacks dogmatic theories, and he only attacks them with dogmatic theories. Accordingly, if the partisans of convention had never claimed an elevated status for custom (as, e.g., the foundation of morality) then the Skeptic would neither question custom, nor oppose custom to nature. If the partisans of sense-perception had never claimed that all perception is true (and so on), then the Skeptic never would have questioned sense-perceptions, nor opposed perceptions to reason. This is stated explicitly at PH I.203, where Sextus explains what he means by saying that "to every argument there is an equal argument opposed"; this means, he says, "to every argument examined by me which establishes a point dogmatically (*hos kataskeuazei ti dogmatikôs*), it seems to me that there is opposed another argument, establishing a point dogmatically (*kataskeuazôn ti dogmatikôs*), which is equal to the first in respect of persuasiveness or dissuasiveness."

As we saw above in the discussion of criteria, it is not sight per se that Sextus calls into question, but rather a certain use of sight, its employment in Dogmatical arguments as a criterion of infallible cognition. Outside of the arguments about the criterion, a parallel point still holds; it is not the senses, or evidence (*to enarges* or *enargeia*) or the *phainomena* that Sextus questions or opposes, but a certain use to which they are put in establishing the Dogmatists' systems.

This accounts for some of the terminological confusion in Sextus; it explains why he sometimes refers to what seems to be a *phainomenon* as though it were an argument put forward to establish something. This can be seen in the *phônê* mentioned above, " to every *logos* there is an equal *logos* opposed". This general statement

14. E.g., PH I.191

is clearly meant to describe every type of skeptical argument (as at PH I.12); and yet it would seem that in many cases what is opposed to a *logos* is not a *logos* but a *phainomenon* or something *enarges*, as when the arguments against motion are opposed to the evidence that things move.

But the point to be noted here is exactly that this evidence is being used by certain Dogmatists to do what, generally speaking, it is not required to do in the course of normal life, e.g. play a role in the foundations of Epicureanism. The *enarges* is being used as an argument, in order to establish something dogmatically. This is why Sextus specifies, in the *phônê* above, that by "*logos*" he is not referring only to things composed of premisses and conclusions, but rather "whatever in any way establishes something dogmatically" (*ton kataskeuazonta ti dogmatikôs... hopôsoun*). It is also why in his discussion of motion, Sextus refers to *enargeia* as a *logos* that demonstrates things (*deiknus*, AM X.62) or that establishes things (AM X.69).

Philologists may be interested to know that this point has even affected the standard text of Sextus. At PH I.33, the Greek manuscripts all have "...to snow's being white, Anaxagoras opposed the argument that snow is frozen water, and that water is black, so that snow as well is black" (*...ho Anaxagoras, tôi leukên einai tên chiona, antetithei hoti hê chiôn hudôr esti pepêgos, to de hudôr esti melan, kai hê chiôn ara melaina estin*). Here it looks as though an argument is being directly opposed to some evidence, i.e. snow's being white, and that Sextus is endorsing this as a model of Skeptical opposition. But there is also an early Latin translation of the Outlines, whose authority is independent of the extant Greek manuscripts, and whose fidelity and literalness are praised by both Teubner editors.[15] The first Teubner editor, Mutschmann, following the "*construenti*" of this translation, supplied the word "*kataskeuazonti*" to read "*...tôi <kataskeuazonti> leukên einai tên chiona...*", i.e. "to the argument demonstrating that snow is white, Anaxagoras opposed...." Heintz, however, argued that Mutschmann's supplement would destroy the emphasis on "der reinen Phänomenalität": "Anaxagoras used his logos to combat the evidence itself, not a philosopher who championed evidence, much less a philosopher who employed a *logos* of his own, as one would have to suppose from *kataskeuazonti*."[16] Mau, in his revision of the Teubner text, follows Heintz, commenting "*<kataskeuazonti> Mutschmanni necessarium non esse Heintz et Philippson mihi persuaserunt.*"

As will be clear from my arguments above, I agree with Mutschmann that the Latin translation has here preserved something that the extant Greek manuscripts lost.[17] Sextus opposes the Anaxagorean *logos*, which establishes something dogmatically via premisses and a conclusion, to another kind of *logos*, which establishes something dogmatically, but not via premisses and a conclusion. Heintz is right about what "*kataskeuazonti*" must mean here, but wrong to think that it is out of place. Just as Sextus does not investigate sight per se, but only its elevation into a criterion of infallible cognition, so too he does not investigate "pure phenomenality", *phainomena* or *enargeia* in general, only their use in arguments, or as arguments, designed to establish dogmatic theories.

After putting forward these arguments that the PH Skeptic is a rustic, Barnes spends the rest of his article cataloguing, almost apologetically, the ways in which Sextus seems urbane, and then, perversely enough, decides that the whole issue must be declared a draw: "…I fear that we must conclude either that PH is not uniformly rustic or else that PH is culpably disingenuous…." I agree that Sextus is not "uniformly rustic"; he does not seem rustic to me at all. The only other evidence for rusticity that Barnes even mentions is the fact that many of the opponents of Pyrrhonism opted for a rustic interpretation (in their tales of cliffs and carts). That may offer some evidence that there were skeptics of this disposition (although ancient controversialists were capable of much distortion), but it offers little evidence of what Sextus himself intended. Indeed, from a famous passage of Diogenes Laertius (IX.62) we know that centuries before Sextus, Aenesidemus was already trying to combat the attribution of rabid skepticism to Pyrrho: "Aenesidemus says that he philosophized according to the suspensive argument, but that he certainly did not undertake each of his actions without foresight". Whether Aenesidemus was himself distorting the facts of Pyrrho's case, or merely trying to combat a perennial misunderstanding, is irrelevant to the present question: the evidence shows that he rejected the rabid interpretation of skepticism. It is clear that Sextus was familiar with such an interpretation of skepticism; it underlies much of his careful, painstak-

15. "*Quo plus in ea Translatione elaborabam*," writes Mutschmann, "*eo magis praestantia eius mihi effulgebat….*" (p. xi). More information about the translation and its author (probably one Niccolò da Reggio) may be found in the introduction to the Teubner edition, as well as in footnote 6 of Schmitt 1983.

ing, alas too often futile attempt to distinguish his own positions on assent, the criterion and so on from incautious assimilation to the rabid view. Far from being evidence that Sextus was a rustic, his attempts to show how his opponents misunderstand him are actually evidence of his urbanity.

PART II: APPEARANCES

Myles Burnyeat, in his article "Can the Sceptic Live his Scepticism?", thinks that the key to repulsing the revisionist interpretation lies in the matter of non-epistemic appearance claims. The assent that the revisionist interpretation attributes to the Skeptic is a normal assent to normal beliefs; when the Skeptic says that the stove seems hot, he means to be making a claim about the stove, not merely about his passing impressions. Burnyeat thinks that such a claim would violate the Skeptic's commitment to universal doubt; if he says that the stove seems hot, he means "it seems hot, but might well not be hot". The difference between these two kinds of claims about something's "seeming" to be the case is commonly labeled a difference between epistemic and non-epistemic appearance-claims; and it is a part of the revisionist interpretation I am advocating that the Sextan Skeptic quite generally is making epistemic appearance-claims when he talks about ordinary matters.

It is just this that Burnyeat denies:

> Sextus is not going out of his way to leave room for a non-dogmatic type of belief about matters of real existence. On the contrary, he says that when as a sceptic he makes statements with the verb "to be", he is to be understood as meaning "to appear" (PH I.135, 198, 200), and he glosses this use of 'to be' at AM XI. 18 in terms which are unmistakably non-epistemic.[18]

When we look at the passages that Burnyeat cites, we do find Sextus emphasizing that he is about to use the word "*esti*" in a non-standard way:

> ...[By the Eighth Mode] we conclude that, since all things are relative, we shall suspend judgement as to what things are existent absolutely and as regards the nature of things. But this point we

16. Studien, p. 6. I have learned a great deal from Heintz' careful textual criticism.
17. As elsewhere; see, e.g., PH I.178,4-5 where the translation restores a line lost to homoioteleuton.

> must notice—that here as in other places we use the term "are" for the term "appear", and what we virtually mean is "all things appear relative." (PH I.135)

> [W]henever the Skeptic says "All things are undetermined," he takes the word "are" in the sense of "appear to him..." (PH I.198)

> We adopt a similar attitude [to that expressed in 198] when we say "All things are non-apprehensible"... so that the meaning expressed is "All...appear to me non-apprehensible" (PH I.200)

> [T]he word 'is' has two meanings, one of these being "really exists" (as, at the present moment, we say "It is day" for "Day really exists"); and the other "appears" (as some of the mathematicians are frequently in the habit of saying that the distance between two stars "is" a cubit's length, this being equivalent to "appears to be but is not really"; for perhaps it is really one hundred stades but appears to be a cubit owing to its height and owing to the distance from the eye). When, then, as Skeptics we say that "of existing things some are good, others evil, others between these two," as the element "are" is twofold in meaning, we insert the "are" as indicative not of real existence but of appearance. (AM XI.18-19)

All four of these quotations claim that "is" is being used in the sense of "appears"; the last of the four is the most explicit in describing exactly what kind of appearance-claims are involved, viz. non-epistemic appearance-claims. Other writers have followed Burnyeat in taking this as a death-blow for the revisionist reading.[19] I do not. Even granting Burnyeat's claim that AM XI.18 shows a non-epistemic sense of "appears", the quotations will not show what he wants them to.

In order to understand the uses of "*phainesthai*" and "*einai*" that Sextus is distinguishing here, we must pay more attention to the contexts of the utterances in which they occur. The first three, from PH I, occur in Sextus' discussion of the skeptical *phônai*, which are meant to summarize and express the results of the Skeptic's investigations. The fourth passage, from AM XI, occurs at the beginning of an investigation, where Sextus is laying out the positions and theories that he intends to examine. In differ-

18. Burnyeat 1980a p. 46.

ent ways, each of these contexts affects the sorts of statements that Sextus wants to make. I shall argue below that his use of "*phainesthai*" and "*einai*" at the beginning of a skeptical investigation is different from his use of it at the end; but that both of them are different from his use of to *phainomenon* as a practical criterion.

I begin by discussing the three passages about the *phônai* from PH I. In order to understand why Sextus feels the need to be clear about his meaning in these passages, one must first make sure of what he is discussing. That is, one must understand what sorts of subjects take this particular use of the verb *esti* here. This is brought out most clearly in the second and third quotations, which clarify the Skeptic's use of the *phônai* "all things are undetermined" and "all things are non-apprehensible". If we include more context around the above quotations, we find that Sextus glosses the phrase "all things" as well as the verb "are":

> Indetermination (*aoristia*) too is a state of mind in which we neither deny nor affirm any of the matters which are subjects of dogmatic inquiry, that is to say, non-evident. So whenever the Skeptic says "All things are undetermined," he takes the word "are" in the sense of "appear to him," and by "*all things*" *he means not everything that there is but such of the non-evident matters investigated by the Dogmatists as he has examined*...so that the statement amounts to this— "*All of the matters of dogmatic inquiry which I have examined* appear to me to be such that no one of them is preferable to the one in conflict with it in respect of credibility or incredibility." (PH I.198-199)

> We adopt a similar attitude [to that expressed in 198-9] when we say "All things are non-apprehensible"...the meaning expressed is "*All of the non-evident matters of dogmatic inquiry which I have investigated* appear to me non-apprehensible." And this is the utterance not of one who is positively asserting that the matters investigated by the Dogmatists are really of such a nature as to be non-apprehensible, but of one who is announcing his own experience, "wherein," he says, "I conceive that up till now I myself have apprehended none of those things owing to the equipollence of

19. e.g. Barnes 1983 fn. 18, p. 11.

> the opposites; and therefore also nothing that is brought forward to overthrow our position seems to me to have any bearing on what we announce." (PH I.200)

The second glosses, I take it, are no less important than the first. He is using a non-epistemic sense of "appear", but he is applying it to the non-evident objects of dogmatic enquiry. And it is reasonable enough that these should be the subject-matter of his *phônai*; for these are exactly the items that he identifies as the object of his continuing search in the first sentences of the Outlines. The phrases "*ta dogmatikôs zêtoumena*" and "*ta para tois dogmatikois zêtoumena*" repeated in both quotations, are modeled on the phrase "*ta kata philosophian zêtoumena*" of PH I.2. The difference is, that where the Skeptic began to investigate and is still investigating, say, the fundamental components of reality, the Platonist has decided that these are Platonic forms, and now directs his investigations to the elucidation of the theory of forms. All parties began by seeking the truth according to philosophy; the Skeptic is still seeking it, but does not take any stand about the items specifically posited by each of the schools after they decided they had found it.

But once we see that the subject of the Skeptic's utterances are exactly such things as Platonic forms and Epicurean atoms, it makes perfect sense that the Skeptic should be reluctant to use the verb "is" in its normal sense about any of these things. For then the Skeptical utterances just become another bit of dogmatic positing, in the following three distinct ways. Platonists think that the forms are unique and unchanging; given the normal sense of "are", their belief can equally be expressed as "we believe that there are such things as forms; and about them we affirm that they have the qualities of uniqueness and unchangeability." If the Skeptic used "are" in the same way, his general utterance "all of the objects of dogmatic enquiry are undetermined" would be equivalent to a series of individual statements "we Skeptics believe that there are such things as Platonic forms (and hylomorphic entelechies, and Epicurean atoms, and so on); and about each of these items we affirm that they have the quality of indeterminateness."[20] Naturally the Skeptic wants to avoid being taken to make this statement; for first it commits him to the existence of non-evident things; and second it commits him to ascribing a real quality to them (notice the qualification that Sextus adds; the Skeptic is not saying that the

Dogmatists' entities are "really of such a nature" as to be non-apprehensible). Third, it commits him to an unskeptical termination of the search for philosophical truth. For if the statement that the objects of dogmatic enquiry are indeterminate is taken as claim about the nature of certain existing things, it seems to rule out permanently the possibility that the Dogmatists might be right, i.e. it seems to be an assertion of the contradictory of the Dogmatists' claims. Whereas it may be that, in the long run, when we have better luck with our enquiries than we have had so far, hylomorphic entities will turn out to be better candidates than they have seemed up till this point; this cannot be ruled out now. The Skeptic is still searching for the truth according to philosophy; he still has an open mind.

The *phônai* , then, cannot tell us about the Skeptic's daily life and reaction to normal situations, just because the *phônai* are statements only about the non-evident objects of dogmatic enquiry. But even that statement is misleading, if one infers from it that there must actually be such non-evident objects for the *phônai* to be statements about, i.e. that the forms, atoms, spermatic formulae and so on must actually exist. It is precisely this misunderstanding that the Skeptic wishes to guard against by saying that the verb "*einai*" in his statements must be understood as though it meant "*phainesthai*" in the non-epistemic sense[21]. The Skeptic wants to sum up the results of his inquiries into the technical philosophies of the schools, and report his impressions of the status of such alleged entities as Epicurean atoms. He wants to say, for instance, that he has not yet been convinced of the claim that there are such things, nor of the Peripatetics' rival claims that there are not. He does not want to go on record as saying that they do not exist, or as saying that they exist but have particular properties (e.g. of being indeterminate or uncognizable), because it may be that on further enquiry he or others will come to decide that they do exist, and find that they are able to make statements about their determinacy and so on. He just wants to say that, so far, he has not found them, or gotten the kind of grasp of them implied by the term "cognition". And he wants to say this in such a way as to avoid appearing, even by the structure of his utterance, to vouch for their existence, or to make any statements about them as though they existed—which can be a difficult thing to do, as is shown by the occurrences of "their", "them" and "they" earlier in this very sentence. The comments about "*einai*" and "*phainesthai*" are his attempt to make clear where his ontological commitments end.

The passage from the beginning of the discussion of ethics in AM XI displays a related, but different, attempt to avoid misunderstanding. The first point to make is that the sentence in which the problematic use of "are" appears is clearly a summary of dogmatic views. In the preface to this work (Against the Ethicists), Sextus says that since Socrates "almost all [sc. of the Dogmatists][22] have with one accord supposed that the study of ethics is concerned with the distinction between things good and evil..."(AM XI.2). Then he begins the work proper by saying:

> All the philosophers who seem to teach systematically the principles [of ethics], and, most notably of all, those of the Old Academy and the Peripatetics, and the Stoics also, are accustomed to make a distinction by saying that "of existing things, some are good, some evil, some between these two," and these last they term "indifferent". (AM XI.3)

Sextus then quotes Xenocrates' peculiar formulation of the same distinction, and in the following eleven sections of AM XI.7-17 he turns aside to canvas various "captious objections" (*heurêsilogia*) that some have put forward against the logical form of this tripartition (e.g. that it does not follow the proper genus-species lines, or commits other logical sins). After this detour, Sextus returns to the thread he had dropped, saying:

> However, there is no necessity now to speak at length about these objections [sc. the captious logical ones]; but it will, perhaps be fitting to explain first that the word "is" (*einai*) has two meanings,

20. Compare this to a position sometimes attributed to Pyrrho himself, according to which statements of indeterminacy have metaphysical, not epistemological, import and application (as e.g. by Bett 1994a, and also see Long & Sedley on Timon apud Aristocles: "We are to take it that indeterminability really is the nature of things", LS I.17). I have argued in Brennan 1998a that the metaphysical interpretation of Pyrrho's skepticism runs directly counter to our best evidence about Pyrrho, and is not supported by any good interpretive arguments. The most that can be said is that certain ancient critics of Pyrrho were not always careful to distinguish the metaphysical from the epistemological view, or wanted to tar the epistemological position with the difficulties attendant on the metaphysical one. But be that as it may, if this sort of position was already attributed to Pyrrho in antiquity, whether rightly or wrongly, the Sextan skeptic would want to distinguish his position from it. The quoted passages can be read as expressing that effort at differentiation.
21. Compare modern comments about how an anthropologist would describe the results of investigating reports of witches or witchcraft.

> one of these being "really exists" (as, at the present moment, we say "It is day" for "Day really exists"); and the other "appears" (*phainesthai*) (as some of the mathematicians are frequently in the habit of saying that the distance between two stars "is" a cubit's length, this being equivalent to "appears to be but is not really"; for perhaps it is really one hundred stades but appears to be a cubit owing to its height and owing to the distance from the eye). When, then, as Skeptics we say that "of existing things some are good, others evil, others between these two," as the element "are" is twofold in meaning, we insert the "are" as indicative not of real existence but of appearance. (AM XI.17-19)

This is the context of the fourth quotation, in which Burnyeat finds the damning evidence of non-epistemic appearances. First, Sextus says "all the philosophers—Old Academics, Peripatetics, Stoics, and Xenocrates—divide things into the good, bad, and indifferent". Then, he parenthetically considers some logical objections to the division. Then, he makes this point about non-standards usage of "*esti*". Finally, he closes the introduction and moves to the next chapter by saying "So, now that the division mentioned above has been posited in the indicated fashion (*keimenês...tês proeirêmenês diaireseôs*), let us see what we ought to think about the things in it, beginning our discussion with the conception [sc. of the good, bad, and indifferent]."

So the statement in which the celebrated "are" occurs ("Of existing things, some are good, others evil, others between these two") is a summary of a position common to all of the professional ethicists, i.e. Dogmatists; and Sextus' explicit gloss on the verb reflects his concern not to be understood as speaking in *propria persona*. As with the earlier *phônai*, Sextus wants to avoid being committed (or appearing to be committed) to the existence and qualities of objects posited by the Dogmatists. Unlike the *phônai*, this

---

22. What is my license for this restriction? Why could not the "all" in "almost all" mean "all human beings quite generally", or "all philosophers, including Sextan Skeptics"? The answer is, first, that it cannot mean all human beings quite generally, since it applies only to those who have a view about the nature and structure of ethical theory; and this surely excludes non-philosophers. But then it also cannot mean "all philosophers, both Dogmatists and Skeptics", because of the word *kai* in the last clause of the sentence; Sextus says that "because almost all" think that ethical theory involves the trichotomy, so "we too" (*kai hêmas*) will have to investigate the trichotomy, i.e. we Skeptics, in addition to everyone mentioned before. So the group referred to as "almost all" must include only Dogmatists; which is immediately confirmed by the words in AM XI.3, quoted next in the main text.

statement does not even represent the Skeptic's report of his experiences, no matter how carefully hedged about; it is merely a statement of the Dogmatists' position, put forward by Sextus in order to have a *dogma* to go to work on. In order to start his discussion rolling, he must refer to the positions of the Dogmatists. And it is their (relatively unanimous) position that things are either good or evil or indifferent. But the Skeptic is not making this statement on his own; so far as his investigative interests go, he is merely entertaining the possibility, not endorsing it. He introduces the Dogmatic trichotomy in order to have the division laid down so that he can begin his Skeptical discussion and investigation. But his own discussion begins only after the positing of the trichotomy, which is not itself part of his Skeptical position. And this should affect the way that we understand the glossing of "*einai*" by the language of non-epistemic appearances, since this glossing occurs in the course of Sextus' introduction of the trichotomy.

This also explains how we should understand the key term "*skeptikôs*", whose import Burnyeat misses. "When as Skeptics we say..." does not mean "when we are doing our grocery-shopping, planning for the future, giving advice to others, and so on"; it means "when we are exercising that peculiar antithetical capacity that makes us Skeptics". As Sextus tells us in PH I. 8-11, what makes a person a Skeptic is the possession of a particular kind of power, which is something akin to the skill possessed by a good boxing promoter: the ability to pick pairs of items which have a fairly even chance of reducing each other to insensibility. This "*dunamis antithetikê*", i.e., this skill in the handling and pairing off of Dogmatical arguments, is all that is implied by the adverb "*skeptikôs*". Sextus must refer to dogmatical opinions in his line of work, but he does not wish to be contaminated by their dogmatism, nor to seem to be contaminated by it; that is why he explicitly dons the sterile garments of non-epistemic talk. But the strict hygiene that he adopts when being a Skeptic—i.e. when exercising his antithetical power—is not carried over to his daily occupations; the antibiotic strain that runs through his discussions of Dogmatists is no proof that his practical beliefs, the beliefs he employs in his daily life when not examining dogmatic systems, are any different from the beliefs of farmers, grocers, and other non-philosophers.

Accordingly, I grant that Sextus does sometimes use "*einai*" to mean "*phainesthai*", and that sometimes when he does so, he means a non-epistemic kind of appearing. But when we see exactly what sort of contexts he does this in, we are no longer tempted to think that the Skeptic always or of necessity talks only about his internal feelings. In particular, Burnyeat's argument that the use of non-epistemic appearance claims rules out the attribution of normal, non-dogmatic beliefs to the Skeptic comes to look like an *ignoratio elenchi*. The revisionist interpretation claims that the Skeptic has normal beliefs, and makes normal appearance-claims, about normal, non-technical issues; evidence that the Skeptic makes peculiar claims about peculiar issues proves nothing to the contrary. It is surely a mistake to generalize from Sextus' use of the language of non-epistemic appearances in his introduction of a Dogmatic division, to the general interpretive conclusion that all of his uses of *einai*, in every context, are non-epistemic appearance-claims.

I anticipate the following objection. I have been arguing that Sextus' use of the non-epistemic sense of "*phainesthai*" here tells us something sensible and predictable about his professional dialectical habits, and nothing about his practical attitudes or his conduct of life. But as the passage at AM XI continues, Sextus makes a comment that my ingenious opponents are sure to seize on. In explaining why he uses "*einai*" in the non-epistemic sense of "*phainesthai*", Sextus says "[f]or concerning the subsistence, as regards the nature of things, of things good and evil and neither, we have contests enough with the Dogmatists; but as regards the appearance of each of these things we are in the habit (*ekhomen ethos*) of designating it good or evil or indifferent...." Now we know that *ethos* is part of the fourfold criterion of observation through which the Sextan Skeptic conducts his life undogmatically; at PH I.24 he tells us that the tradition of laws and customs (*paradosis ethôn kai nomôn*) is that "whereby we regard piety in the conduct of life as good, but impiety as bad." Here in AM XI, he is telling us that it is part of the Skeptical *ethos* to say that things are good or bad or indifferent, and explicitly glossing that "are" as non-epistemic. These judgments of value are made in accordance with the Skeptical *ethos*; these judgements are non-epistemic, therefore judgements made in accordance with the Skeptical ethos are non-epistemic judgements. But the Skeptical *ethos* is one of the four criteria of practical action; therefore practical action, and thus all of the Skeptic's attitudes and beliefs, involve non-epistemic judgements—not merely those involving Dogmatical theories[23].

Thus runs my opponents' objection. But it seems to me misplaced, for it cannot explain the following passages, which show us what the "Skeptical *ethos*" here alluded to really is. Summing up the opposing arguments about the indicative sign, Sextus comments as follows:

> ...[A]t this point it is right to keep in mind the habit of the Sceptics (*to skeptikon ethos*). This is to set out the arguments against the existence of the sign, but not with conviction or assent (for to do it in that way would be equivalent to maintaining that a sign exists, like those who dogmatize), but so as to bring the enquiry to a position of equipollence....And now that the habit of the Sceptics has been set forth (*tou skeptikou ethous parastathentos*), let us next proceed to develop the theme before us (AM VIII.159-161).

Again, at the beginning of his discussion of place (*topos*), he says

> Having explained the conception of place and indicated the matters connected with it [i.e. void and room], it remains for us to set in motion the arguments on either side and confirm the suspension introduced about them—which is the habit of the Skeptics (*hôs estin ethos tois apo tês skepseôs*) (AM X.6).

Sextus is very clear that the Skeptical *ethos* he is reminding us of in this case is a habit of argumentation, namely, the opposing of Dogmatical arguments without subscribing to either side. For my opponents to maintain that the "Skeptical *ethos*" described here has anything to do with the "*ethê kai nomoi*" mentioned in the criterion of action would obviously be implausible. With these passages in mind,[24] we can see that the passage from AM XI is referring to exactly the same thing. That is, that when Sextus there says "we have the habit of saying that things are good bad and indifferent, meaning by this only that they appear so but may not be so", he is simply referring again to the fact that he is putting forth the Dogmatists' trichotomy as part of his antithetical project, without subscribing to its truth.

This is also brought out by the parenthetical remark in the above quotation from AM VIII.159, "*ison gar ên to toiouto poiein, tôi axioun einai ti sêmeion paraplêsiôs tois dogmatizousin*". Sextus is concerned that even arguments against the existence of the sign, if understood as having been put forward with assent (*meta peismatos kai sugkatatheseôs*), might commit him to a Dogmatical position, namely the Dogmatical denial of the existence of signs.[25] At every stage in his Skeptical activities, Sextus is conscious that his behavior is open to misconstruction; the very argument that he makes in order to bring about *isostheneia* may be mistakenly construed as an act of dogmatically denying existence; the very act of raising a view for discussion may be misconstrued as a Dogmatical assertion of view in question. It is exactly this wary circumspection that is at work in Sextus' introduction of the trichotomy of good, bad and indifferent; in the interests of making clear that he is merely summarizing the Dogmatic position and does not want to be committed to it, he puts to use the same device for limiting commitments that we saw him using in the *phônai*.

Once we see how the non-epistemic appearance claims function in the *phônai*, we can also grasp the significance of missing context in other parts of Burnyeat's article. For instance,[26] in arguing that the Skeptic cannot have ordinary beliefs, Burnyeat quotes PH I.15 in the form, "He states what appears to himself and announces his own experience without belief, making no assertion about external things." But the actually passage begins a few words earlier: "And, what is most important, in the uttering of the *phônai* [which Sextus has just been discussing] he states...". The restriction of scope carries over; the *phônai* register his experiences in studying Dogmatical philosophical systems; they do not register his experiences with things in the rest of his life.

CONCLUSION

In the preceding pages I have presented some suggestions about how we ought to understand Sextus' talk of criteria and appearances. In the process, I have also examined several arguments that claim to show that the Sextan Sceptic cannot consistently have ordinary beliefs. I maintain that these arguments do not

23. So far as syllogisms go (this one is roughly an instance of Darapti), the only valid conclusion from the preceding two premisses is the weaker one, that *some* judgements made in accordance with the Skeptical ethos are non-epistemic judgements, and accordingly that *some* of the skeptic's practical attitudes involve non-epistemic judgements. And with this I have no quarrel; since some non-epistemic judgements are embedded in everyone's practical attitudes (e.g., not trying to reach through mirrors), I am happy to suppose that the Sextan skeptic has them, too. But so far as interpretational disputes go, my opponents will surely not be content with the particular.

succeed. Showing that the rabid interpretation as a whole does not succeed is of course another matter; and showing that the revisionist interpretation improves on it, still a third; the resolution of the critical dispute must wait for further contributions from both sides. In the meantime, I hope that my positive suggestions will constitute a contribution to our understanding of Sextus, no matter which overall interpretation we eventually decide to adopt.

POSTSCRIPT 1999

By offering to reprint my article, the editors of *Acta Philosophica Fennica* gave me an opportunity to clarify my position on the crucial passage from AM XI.19, the statement of the axiological trichotomy in which Sextus claims to use "*einai*" to mean "*phainesthai*". In the original version of this paper, I described Sextus' relation to this statement as one of "quoting", i.e. that in saying that "some things are good, etc.", Sextus was quoting the Dogmatists as saying "some things are good, etc." Sextus certainly does sometimes quote the Dogmatists in this way, e.g. AM XI.4, where he writes "Xenocrates was in the habit of saying 'each being is either good or bad or neither good nor bad' (*Xenokratês...ephaske*)." Here we have quotation properly speaking.

However, by describing Sextus' comment at AM XI.19 as a case of quotation, I invited the following objection, brought to my attention by John Cooper, which I included as a footnote in the

24. Two more may be found at AM IX.312 (hôs ethos tois apo tês skepseôs) and AM VII. 443 (skeptikon ethos). There is a fifth, I believe, but it occurs in a vexed passage. At AM VII.435, the manuscripts have "paresti de, ei tini philon esti [to prolong the argument], kai tas allas aporias ton anterôtônta, hôs ethos ekhousin autois tois skeptikois proagein." Most editors assume some corruption and a lacuna, and make various conjectures. I am happy to find myself in agreement with Bekker, who conjectured "...aporias <komisai> ton anterôtônta, has ethos echousin autois [viz., tois Stôikois] hoi skeptikoi proagein." The predictability of the error, and the many parallel passages—one only eight sections later—make the emendation quite certain, in my view.

25. I take this opportunity of confessing, to my embarrassment, that I have misdescribed this passage three times. In each of the earlier incarnations of this piece, I took it that "*ison gar ên to toiouto poiein, tôi axioun einai ti sêmeion*" meant that Sextus was concerned that his argument against the existence of the sign, if understood in a certain way, would actually commit him to the existence of the sign. This was to read "*ison*" in a natural way, but it gave Sextus a strange view about the equivalence of two arguments, that an argument for not-P would somehow commit him to P. What I did not then see is that "*ison*" ought to be understood in light of the final qualification "*paraplêsiôs tois dogmatizousin*", so as to mean something like "equally dogmatical". Then the point is not literal identity of conclusion (that his counter argument against the existence of signs would still somehow produce the conclusion that signs exist), but rather something like the "moral equivalence" of two kinds of dogmatizing.

original paper.[27] If Sextus were actually quoting the trichotomy, i.e. explicitly attributing these very words to the Dogmatists, and uttering them only for the purpose of making the attribution, then he ought not also to say that the word "*einai*" is being used in some special, Skeptical way within the quotation. He ought not to, because to do so would actually distort the contents of the quotation, and attribute Skeptical terminology to its Dogmatic authors. Conversely, were it really a proper quotation, Sextus would not need to offer any special plea, since the mere fact that it was a quotation would exculpate the Skeptic from any dogmatical entanglements. Thus it cannot be right to say, as I did, both that Sextus is quoting, and that Sextus uses "*einai*" in a non-standard way in order to avoid the appearance of commitment to the contents of the quotation.

This objection has always struck me as interesting and important, but not insurmountable. It requires some alteration of my position, but does not change the basic facts about the texts in hand, each of which seems to me fully secured by evidence:

1) The trichotomy is introduced as a piece of Dogmatic theory, attributed to certain named Dogmatic schools (AM XI.3-4), and more generally to everyone who has a view about the theoretical structure of ethics, i.e. all Dogmatists (AM XI.2).
2) The sole point of its introduction is to allow Sextus to begin practicing his Skeptical method on it, i.e. producing aporiai, raising objections, inquiring, and investigating. This is emphasized at the beginning in AM XI.2, where Sextus says that it is because the Dogmatists subscribe to the trichotomy that he will be required to investigate it (*all' epei...deêsei kai hêmas...skopein*). It is again emphasized at the end of our chapter (AM XI.20), when Sextus says "now that the aforementioned division has been posited, let us see what we ought to think about its contents". At no point in the intervening sections would Sextus have felt called upon to make a personal statement of his own views on the foundations of axiology; indeed, such an interjection of his own views would have been quite irrelevant to the project he has in hand, namely that of setting out a Dogmatic distinction for

26. Burnyeat 1980a p. 136.

the purpose of investigating it.

3) All of this is confirmed by his reference to the "Skeptical habit" or ethos in AM XI.20. The passages adduced above (AM VIII.159-161, AM X.6, AM IX.312, AM VII. 443, and possibly AM VII.435) show beyond doubt that the "Skeptical habit" to which Sextus is referring here is an argumentative habit, involving the positing and deployment of arguments and objections, couched in Dogmatical language, but without any commitment to Dogmatical views. It is simply standard Sextan procedure, here and elsewhere, to begin with a summary exposition of the dogmatical views to be considered.
4) Despite the fact that Sextus does not utter the trichotomy in propria persona, he is clearly concerned that he may appear to be committed to it, as we can tell both from the comments about "*einai*" and "*phainesthai*", and from the fragment of Timon in AM XI.20. Since I said nothing about this fragment in my original article, I hope I may be excused for commenting on it at some length now.

It is fairly clear that Sextus introduces the fragment of Timon here exactly to show how Skeptics can use the language of appearance in order to disown statements that would otherwise sound dogmatic.[28] In this fragment, Pyrrho seems to claim access to the truth about the nature of the divine and of goodness—a deeply dogmatic claim to make. But he precedes these statements with the word "*kataphainetai*", and this, Sextus seems to think, makes all the difference.

According to the current critical consensus, it does not. Several recent interpreters have shown that there is no way to understand the fragment in a natural way, and still integrate its contents with Pyrrho's otherwise Skeptical outlook; *kataphainetai* or no, the content is irredeemably dogmatic. Burnyeat tried to reconstrue the Greek in a forced and implausible way, and even then could show only meager philosophical improvements in Pyrrho's consistency.[29] Bett[30] detailed the inadequacy of Burnyeat's view, while further demonstrating how the contents of the fragment are not consistent with Pyrrho's position; in par-

27. Bett 1997 p. 60 refers to the version of this chapter that appeared as Brennan 1994, repeats Cooper's objection without attributing it to Cooper, and does not answer the replies that I made in Brennan 1994.

ticular he argued that *kataphainetai* could not have been used in Timon's time to mean what Sextus wants it to mean. But Bett then leapt to the extraordinary conclusion that the speaker must not be Pyrrho, or Timon, or any other authoritative Skeptic! This makes nonsense of the passage, since Sextus quotes Timon solely for the reason—and with this analysis Bett agrees—that the quotation offers some palliation and precedent for Sextus' own apparent misstep into Dogmatic pronouncement. The speaker in Timon's fragment says prima facie dogmatic things, but precedes them all with the word *kataphainetai*, which Sextus takes to mean something like "non-epistemically appears", and so the speaker is absolved of the dogmatic stigma. And if Timon's speaker can say dogmatic-sounding things, and yet not be dogmatic, then so can Sextus, by the same method of converting it all into talk about appearances. But notice that, on this understanding of the fragment's role in the passage, Sextus will have used the quotation as license for his language, only because he understood it to originate in the mouth of a speaker whose usage sets a pattern for later Pyrrhonists. Sextus excuses his non-Skeptical sounding language by saying that "even Timon" says these sorts of things—and whether he means by this Timon himself, or (more likely) Timon quoting his master Pyrrho, the point will be that this sort of linguistic laxity can be found in the mouths of even the most scrupulous Skeptics. Not in the mouth of a non-Skeptic, or an opponent of Pyrrho, or Timon before his conversion, as Bett suggests—if Sextus had thought the fragment's words issued from any such non-authoritative mouth, then he never would have quoted it in his own support. Sextus, who had the poem before him, thought the speaker was an authoritative Pyrrhonian, presumably Pyrrho himself, and barring papyrological epiphanies we will never be in a position to contradict him.

So the fragment of Timon again shows Sextus' concern not to be understood as committed to the trichotomy. But this is not because—as Burnyeat might argue—Sextus universally and on all topics wants to avoid commitments of any kind. Rather, it is because Sextus is once again practicing his Skeptical *dunamis*, pair-

28. This is Bett's view in Bett 1994b pp. 314-315; "[Sextus] introduces the lines precisely in order to illustrate the sceptic's practice of referring to the way things appear....Sextus takes the words "*hôs moi kataphainetai einai*" as modifying what would otherwise be a statement about the real nature of the divine and the good, converting it instead into a statement palatable to the sceptic...."

ing off Dogmatic arguments one against the other. What Sextus himself thought about goods, bads, and indifferents is left completely undetermined by this passage; if I am right elsewhere, then he will presumably have thought about them exactly what any normal, non-philosophical person in the street thinks, but all that is irrelevant to this stretch of argumentation.

5) It is worth looking again at AM VIII.159, in which Sextus discusses the "skeptical *ethos*" in the course of arguing against the existence of signs. Here too he describes his activity as one of merely setting out or exposing (*ektithesthai*) the arguments for and against the existence of signs, in order to bring the investigation to a state of equipollence (*hôste eis isostheneian tên zêtêsin agein*). And here too he is concerned that unless he explicitly distances himself from the arguments, by saying that he sets them out "without conviction or assent", he may be thought guilty of dogmatizing. It thus provides a close parallel to Sextus' concern, in our current passage, to distance himself from the content of his summary of the Dogmatists' trichotomy.
6) If I am right about the evidence so far, then our only remaining interpretive job is that of providing an accurate description of Sextus' relation to the trichotomy, since I concede that "quotation" is an inaccurate description. In revising the main text, I changed that word at every instance to "summary", and this strikes me as more nearly satisfactory; we might also say "hypothesizing" or "positing", since this word (*keisthai*, i.e. *tithesthai* in the passive) is used in AM XI.20. Sextus needs to interact with the trichotomy in whatever minimal way will place it before his readers and make it a subject for Skeptical investigation.

Note in particular that the central problem with describing it as "quotation" was that this made the non-standard sense of "*einai*" redundant; the work of distancing Sextus from the trichotomy was being done twice over. But more important than looking for an improved label—e.g. "summary", "positing" or what will you—that will avoid this belt-and-suspenders situation, I would like to

29. Burnyeat 1980b.
30. Bett 1994b.

emphasize that the job of distancing is done only once, not by the label that we apply, but exactly by Sextus' comments about "*einai*". He wants to be able to describe his relation to a proposal under investigation, a trichotomy of Dogmatic origin, which, as a Skeptic, he is committed to examining with complete impartiality. So he tries to set out the proposal, without subscribing to it or assenting to its propositional content, in order to proceed to entertain the possibility of its being correct or not, and investigate into "what one should think about it" (*ha khrê phronein*, AM XI.20). It is in this context that, having made the statement that "of things, some are good, etc.", he proceeds to distance himself from any appearance of assertion.

This is the attitude that Sextus takes towards issues of theoretical philosophy. It has been the purpose of this paper to argue that there is no reason to think that he takes this attitude towards other aspects of his life, and in particular no reason to think that every time he utters the verb "*einai*" in the course of his life he is actually making a non-epistemic appearance claim.

Chapter Four

Details of Sextus' Epistemology

An account of Sextus' views on epistemology ought to tell us about such things as dogma, assent, the clear and the unclear, and suspension. I have already mentioned, in the course of the last chapter, how I understand his distinction between two kinds of criterion; in this chapter I shall also explain what Sextus means by distinguishing two kinds of dogmatizing, two kinds of being persuaded (*peithesthai*), and two kinds of *hairesis*. But as often in interpretive debates, the familiar texts in which these distinctions are made have failed to yield unambiguous support for either camp.[1] So in an attempt to shed fresh light on the subject, I shall also discuss Sextus' distinction of two kinds of grammar, two kinds of hellenism, two kinds of astronomy, two ways that numbers exist, and two ways of resolving sophisms.

I begin from the conclusions of the prior chapter. The *dogmata* that form the object of the skeptic's attack are the scientific and technical tenets and pronouncements of the schools; the content of his beliefs in matters of practical activity is not limited to non-epistemic appearance-claims.

If these conclusions are accepted, it seems to me that we should also redraw the scope of *epokhê*. First of all, we should conclude that *epokhê* is a feature of the Skeptic's professional life, as a skeptic, and so extends to those matters that he investigates professionally.[2] The gloss that "*panta*" is given in the skeptical *phônê* at

1. This reception, alas, has met Frede 1984; my work is to that extent an attempt to shore up and extend his conclusions.

2. Given this emphasis on *epokhê* as a feature of the Skeptic's professional life, in what sense can

PH I. 198—"*panta de legei [ho Skeptikos] ou ta onta, all' haper diexelthe tôn para tois dogmatikois zêtoumenôn adêlôn*"—which he then invites us to apply to other *phônai* in PH I.201,[3] should be understood also with the motto of "*epokhê peri pantôn*" (PH I.205, 1.3 1).

I also advocate another divergence from the standard view of *epokhê*, as described by Donald Morrison:

> As I see it, ancient skepticism is essentially a pervasive state of mind and character—namely, the suspension of judgment with regard to all matters, or *epokhê*—-which is induced by a certain fundamental formative experience—namely, being repeatedly persuaded by equally strong arguments first for and then against a series of propositions drawn from across the entire range of possible objects of judgment, or, in Greek, *isostheneia*. This fundamental formative experience, being subjected to equally persuasive arguments pro or con, leads to a pervasive change in one's state of mind and character, global suspension of judgment .... [After someone listens to skeptical arguments, his] mind is so battered by this hammering that he loses his disposition to believe anything.[4]

It should already be clear that I dissent from the equation of *epokhê* with suspension about all matters, simpliciter; that it is not pervasive in this way is crucial to my view. But I also disagree with this account of how *epokhê* comes about, and what it produces, in whatever scope we allow it. On Morrison's picture, skepticism induces a kind of intellectual debility, a crippling of the faculty of assent. The skeptic has suffered, and inflicts on others, a process roughly analogous to bending a stiff wire back and forth until it breaks. The skeptic's victim is successively persuaded of each position and its opposite, worked one way and another until his mind can no longer take on any bent at all. Not a pretty picture, but fair-

the Skeptic and the ordinary person be united in *epokhê*, and jointly contrasted with the Dogmatist and his *sunkatathesis*, as the diagram on p. 6 represents them? For surely "those from life" cannot be said to be in the same state of suspense about, e.g. the analysis of the conditional, as the Skeptic is—they will presumably never have thought about it at all. But they are both alike in not having a dogmatic view about it, and so are properly contrasted with the Dogmatist; the difference between them is only one of familiarity, as I explain in the next chapter. I thank André Laks for raising this point.

3. After Sextus glosses "*panta*" in the context of the *phônê* "*panta estin aorista*" (quoted above), he then begins his explication of the next *phônê* "*panta estin akatalêpta*" by saying "*kai gar to 'panta' homoiôs exêgoumetha*" (PH I.200).

4. Morrison 1990.

ly representative of how suspension is understood on the traditional interpretation.

But it seems to me to lack support at several crucial points. For one thing, there is no reason to believe that the skeptic ever is persuaded at all. Far from being "repeatedly persuaded ... first for and then against", it seems to me that the skeptic never really feels much of a tug from either side of the debate. And I take it that this is the case both on some particular occasion, and over the course of the skeptic's life history. On some particular occasion, for example when investigating whether numbers are elements of the universe or not (PH III.152), it seems to me quite unlikely that the Skeptic first feels fully convinced that the Pythagoreans are right to think that numbers are *stoicheia*, and then persuaded that the contradictory of their position is right. Nor, in the course of the Skeptic's life, is there any reason to suppose that the proto-Skeptic first took on a doctrinal allegiance, and then rejected it. It may be that some people who later became Skeptics had first been, e.g. Stoics. Indeed, members of the dogmatical schools are the Skeptic's primary audience; for it is they who are suffering from the distress peculiar to dogmatism, and so are most in need of the skeptical cure (PH III. 280-281). But in the Skeptic's own life history, detailed at PH I.12, there is no mention of a period of allegiance to a school.[5]

Indeed, there is no reason to see *epokhê* as the outcome of any process of privation of belief at all; the mature skeptic may have no fewer beliefs than at any previous time in his life. I say more about the role of belief conservation in the next chapter.

The second dogma about Sextan skepticism that I wish to modify, if not refute, is that it attacked all forms of belief, where its modern homonyms focus only on knowledge. This is obviously related to the first dogma; it is because the scope of skeptic scrutiny is overextended that the consequences are overestimated. As I understand it, Sextan skepticism was directed only at claims to certain kind of beliefs, or at beliefs that were put forward with certain kinds of claims to be able to justify them. Sextus' typical targets are various brands of technical logic, criteria of infallible first principles, incorrigible sense-perceptions, direct intuition of spooky entities, and so on. Now, it is true that his term for these denizens of scientifico-philosophical theories and frameworks is "*dogmata*";

5. See further in the next chapter.

and it is certainly most accurate to translate this as "belief', not "knowledge". But even those who will disagree with me about most aspects of Sextan skepticism, will agree that the Greek term "*dogma*" tends to pick out beliefs that have a certain status, particularly because of their place within a system.[6] And I will try to show that, in fact, what makes something a *dogma* in the Sextan sense is exactly its being put forward by its proponent as part of a fully-worked out, justified theory. Beliefs that are not put forward in this way are not subject to skeptical scrutiny.

Accordingly, the target of the Sextan skeptic is not just any claim to a true belief, but claims to certain kinds of true, justified beliefs. This emphasis on justification obviously brings Sextus' target much closer to the modern target of knowledge. It would still not be true to say that Sextus challenges all and only claims to knowledge, as might some modern skeptic; even if one is willing to identify knowledge with true justified belief, the picture is still more complicated than that (as I shall soon show). But given this much, it should be obvious why I cannot agree that the ancient skeptic made no distinction between belief and knowledge and attacked both indiscriminately.

Some claims to knowledge, I suspect, would not have been challenged by Sextus because they are made undogmatically and in accordance with the conduct of life or of the crafts. For instance, when physicians assess the mental status of a patient who has suffered a lapse of consciousness, it is customary for them to note whether the patient knows what day it is, and knows their own (i.e. the patient's) name. If in this circumstance a physician were to say, "Well, the patient seems confused about what day it is, but he still knows his name", there is no reason to think that the Skeptic would feel compelled to grill either the physician or the patient about this claim to knowledge. Of course, special circumstances might cast some practical doubt on the matter if, e.g., the patient was completely anonymous and had no documentary records; but these sorts of doubts also generally suggest practical means of resolution, quite unlike universal skeptical doubts. Indeed, not only would the skeptic not question such a claim to knowledge, he would probably even make such claims himself. For instance, if it were Sextus himself who had examined the patient and was now

6. See footnote 8 of Chapter 3.

reporting on him, it would obviously be grossly misleading for him to deny that the patient knew his name. He could not practice medicine according to the teachings of the craft, if when another physician asked about the mental status of a patient he were to reply, "He suspended judgment about the day, and he had a rash and headlong conviction about his name, but given how little he has thought about the problem of the criterion, not to mention the controversy over the valid conditional, he clearly does not know his name." If we take Sextus at his word, when he says that one of his practical criteria is the *didaskalia technôn* (PH I.24), then we must suppose that he will sometimes attribute knowledge to people. And this should not trouble us; when Sextus is exercising his medical capacity, he is presumably not also exercising his antithetical capacity.

There are thus certain situations in which it is customary to make and accept knowledge claims on the sorts of grounds envisioned above, and there is no reason to think that the Sextan skeptic would not follow these customs, too.[7] This is part of why I denied above that the Sextan skeptic will challenge all and only knowledge-claims; he will not challenge all of them. There are two further reasons why I hesitate to say that he challenges only claims to knowledge. One is that I am personally unconvinced that knowledge is true justified belief, and even less persuaded that Sextus would endorse that analysis. Another, related reason is that notions like challenging, doubting, scrutinizing, and so on are obviously intentional notions; they defy substitution of equivalents, even if all parties are agreed on the correct analysis. If we want to know what Sextus challenged, doubted, and so on, then part of what we want to know about is the description under which he challenged the things he challenged. In discussing Sextus, one of my main tasks is to provide a coherent characterization and analysis of those items that were, in fact, the objects of his skeptical endeavors. But even if that analysis shows the items to be equivalent to knowledge in our theories, or even (per impossible) in Sextus' own theories, it would still be a mistake to conclude that the skeptic challenged, doubted, and so on, claims to knowledge. Sextus himself most commonly

7. Notice that it would be misleading to say that there are certain situations in which one is justified in making knowledge claims based on the grounds envisioned above, unless one then distinguished types of justification.

talks about "*dogmata*", and that is most accurately translated "beliefs". Even as I describe the kind of belief claims he challenged, and argue that he challenged only claims to a certain kind of justified true belief, I am still not arguing that he challenged only knowledge claims.

Concerns about analyses to one side, however, I hope it is clear why the current shibboleth, that moderns challenge only knowledge where ancients challenged all belief, must be modified to the extent that we refine our understanding of Sextus' use of "*dogmata*".

And in any case, there is something a bit perverse about the whole comparison; modern skepticism presumably argues that we do not in fact know some or all of the things that we believe we know; what is the ancient version meant to be: that we do not in fact believe some or all of the things that we believe we believe? Again, the key is justification; what the ancient skeptic questions are claims to believe something on the basis of a criterion of *katalêpsis*. *Katalêpsis* is assent to an impression that is not merely veridical, but could not be otherwise than veridical; if things were not as the impression represents them, then one would not be having this impression. Given that this sort of belief is the object of ancient skeptical enquiry, it is surely very misleading to say that they attacked all belief, and not merely knowledge.

In relation to *katalêpsis*, it is useful to note that two features of Sextan skepticism, the attacks on the clarity of sense-perception, and the reliance on the disagreement between individuals (*diaphônia*), make a lot more sense if one keeps in mind the generally empiricist epistemological climate of the times. Most of the important figures of ancient Pyrrhonism—Pyrrho himself, Arcesilaus and Carneades, Aenesidemus, Agrippa and Sextus, fall into the period between Plato's advocacy of nonsensory perception of forms, and the neo-Platonist revival of similar theories in the third century A.D. Of course there are immensely important differences between empiricism in the Stoics, Epicureans and Peripatetics, but there are also similarities, which we can add up into a sort of composite sketch of the Pyrrhonist's opponents. According to this the mind begins as a tabula rasa, and develops all of its concepts either directly by running into the objects as given in sense-perception (*kata periptôsin*), or by a few familiar means of abstraction from those first-order concepts—similarity, analogy, negation, and so on.[8] All deductions, whether via Aristotelian syllogisms or Stoic propositional logic, take these concepts so-derived as their input. The Epicureans, who avoid any formal logic but are still concerned with drawing inferences, are even more explicit about the fact that all inference is just the articulation of our primary concepts given to us by sense perception. It is built into each of these systems that it is our direct sense-perception of individuals that provides the grounding for inferential chains of whatever length; they do not merely want to say that our ability to see things in front of our face is generally reliable and handy for getting around, they want to say that it has a particular status in grounding comprehensive theories of everything, theories that are then justified in overturning ordinary beliefs at will. When Sextus questions the validity of sense-perception, he is not questioning whether it can give us any better reason to leave by the door than the window, but whether it can play this foundational role in dogmatic systems. And the mode of disagreement between individuals is important exactly because, given theories of concept-formation like these, which posit a sequence of physical events guaranteed to provide us with concepts adequate to the understanding of everything, it is hard to account for the fact that fully adult, non-impaired humans can disagree about things. Obviously it is possible for empiricist theories to say more in their defense about the sources of error; but Sextus' attacks on sense-perception are best understood as challenges to do exactly that. To put it in Sextus' own terms, he does not examine sense-perception as a criterion of action, but rather as a criterion of *katalêpsis*, that is, incorrigible truth.

When thinking about what things Sextus does and does not believe, it may be useful to keep in mind the fact that nowhere in any of his writings does Sextus say that he does not know something. There is a fairly standard way to say "I do not know" in Greek—*ouk oida*— and that phrase appears only once in Sextus (AM VII.264), attributed to Socrates (in an odd misquotation of the *Phaedrus*). What Sextus says rather often, and what is something taken as a denial of knowledge, is rather a phrase that we might

8. Nearly identical lists are given by Diogenes Laertius both for the Stoics (D.L. VII. 52-53) and for the Epicureans (D.L. X.32). Similar lists can also be found in Sextus at AM I.25, AM III.40, AM VIII.56-60, AM IX.390 et seq. and AM XI.250 et seq., sometimes in contexts that clearly suggest one school or another as their origin.

translate "I do not cognize", in order to bring out the fact that this is a bit of technical jargon. Cognizing, or *katalêpsis*, is performing the mental act of assent in response to a *kataleptic* impression, that is, an impression which comes from something that exists and represents the thing according to its existence, and in such a way that it could not be false. From that definition, one can see that engaging in talk of "cognizing" means accepting a lot of machinery; impressions, representation, assent, and so on. If you ask me whether I know that there is a table in front of me, then I will be inclined to say yes; if you ask me whether I cognize that there is a table in front of me, then I may feel a certain reluctance even to accept the presuppositions that would allow me to say yes or no. Cognition plays a certain role in Stoicism; it generates the principles on which all inferential chains rest, and thus stands at the bottom of the justificational heap. If you ask me whether I intend to ascribe that kind of status to my belief that there's a table in front of me, the answer is no; when in the nonphilosophical course of events I say that I know there is a table in front of me, I am not positing the existence of the table in this way. Of course, neither am I attempting to refute its existence, either. Now if the Stoics are right, then we cognize things all of the time, from childhood up. It certainly doesn't seem obvious that we do this, but on the other hand it may be that I am cognizing things without being aware of it. Maybe that is the right account of what I do, one that I shall eventually come to believe is right as my enquiries continue. But for the meantime, if somebody asks me whether I am cognizing something, then I have to say that to the extent I understand the question, the answer is that I am certainly not aware of doing so. Here is how Sextus puts it: "The utterance "I am not cognizing" is expressive of a personal feeling (*pathous oikeiou esti dêlôtikê*), according to which the skeptic refrains for the meanwhile from either positing or refuting one of the unclear objects of enquiry."

Refraining from positing things, i.e. claiming to cognize them, is refraining from engaging in a particular set of conventions, bound up with extensive epistemological presuppositions. One might paraphrase the skeptic's utterance by saying, "I do not do cognitions"; the whole theory just has a lot bound up with it that seems to require further investigation. But of course, saying that one does not do cognitions is consistent with knowing things, and with claiming to know things, just as it is perfectly possible to feel that one ought to do something, without accepting the whole framework of categorical imperatives.

But the story of *katalêpsis* or cognition has an interesting epilogue, which I think is also useful for understanding what the Skeptic can believe. I have argued that the Skeptic can believe anything that other people believe, just the way that they believe it, and that what the skeptic refrains from getting involved in are the dogmatic positings of the professional philosophers. But what if, for one reason or another, the technical jargon of the schools becomes part of the general vocabulary of everyday life, and perhaps even shapes the general outlooks of everyday life? What if last year's dogma becomes this year's convention? I maintain that the skeptic should not feel any discomfort at this prospect at all. The most common modern Greek word for "to understand" (*katalavainô*) is a derivative of "*katalêpsis*"; what was the technical Stoic jargon is now just how you say that you "get" something. Surely a modern Sextan will not now avoid saying the Greek equivalent of "I cognize", when this has simply become the way that everyone talks in normal life.[9] More importantly, I think that the Sextan skeptic will have a different attitude towards the Epicurean philosopher's claim that there are atoms, and a twentieth-century schoolchild's utterance of the same words. This is very hard to make clear, but I think that what I want to say is that the content of a dogma can fossilize into convention and ordinary usage; and as it changes its status, or the status of the assertion in which it's put forward, the Skeptic's reaction to it will change as well. This is certainly true about linguistic matters, such as the evolution of "*katalêpsis*" from Stoic jargon to common usage; but I think it is a consequence of my picture of Sextan skepticism that it is equally true of matters of substance. The skeptic only responds to dogmatic positings; but the way in which a school-child comes home from school and shows off their new knowledge that there are atoms does not count as an act of dogmatic positing. The school-child does not believe for the same kinds of reasons, or in the same way, that the Epicurean does. The Epicurean offers justifications for their belief, and the belief has a certain status and role within their comprehensive system; none of this is true of the school-child. It

9. It is interesting to note in this light that the New Testament contains uses of "*kathêkein*" (e.g. "*poiein ta mê kathêkonta*") that are unparalleled in earlier non-technical sources, and may be popularizations of Stoic vocabulary. See, e.g., Acts XXII.22.

would be most accurate, indeed, to say that the child offers no justifications at all for believing it. But it is just this fact that makes the child an ineligible target for the Sextan skeptic altogether. In fact, Sextus uses an illustration rather like this to distinguish the acceptable and unacceptable kinds of believing or being persuaded:

> For the word "to be persuaded" (*peithesthai*) has different meanings; it means not to resist but simply to follow without any strong impulse or inclination, as the boy is said to be persuaded by his tutor; but sometimes it means to assent to a thing of deliberate choice and with a kind of sympathy due to strong desire, as when the incontinent man believes the person who approves an extravagant mode of life. (PH I.230)

The unacceptable kind of being persuaded is like that of an immoralist listening to someone who encourages his inclinations; he deliberately assents to the justification of what he already violently wanted to believe, he assents by choice and with a kind of identification with the belief. But the skeptic follows things or believes things just in the sense that he does not resist them; he does not add any imported vehemence, but just is persuaded by them, the way a child believes its teacher.

This seems to me a very important passage for understanding the skeptic's attitude towards non-philosophical beliefs. He does not scrutinize every kind of belief that he encounters, or every statement that he hears; for the most part he just accepts things. And this doesn't mean that he only accepts them on the surface but doesn't really believe them, that he is still striving for some odd attenuated version of normal beliefs. For that is surely not what the school-child does. The school-child is not some kind of clever chameleon, effecting a mere superficial conformity with his surroundings, or pretending to act as if he believed that Edinburgh is the capital of Scotland, while internally noting only that he is having an impression as of someone telling him that Edinburgh is the capital of Scotland, and refusing to give it any credence until it has passed the test of indubitability. Surely this cannot be right. He just believes it, without any conscious justification at all, and without any feeling that justification is required.

That is the model that the Skeptic adopts. The habit of justification was originally introduced by the positive philosophers themselves, when they first began to think that they could produce systems of such generality and power that they could bring order into the chaos of ordinary belief, revising or discarding existing beliefs if they did not meet the standards of their theories, and improving the existing beliefs that were retained, by showing how they fit into the correct theory. Outside of the sphere of philosophy, or dogmatism, as Sextus refers to it, people just believe things, for all sorts of reasons, good and bad, and sometimes for no reason at all. This is what Sextus refers to as believing things undogmatically.

But the traditional interpretation, mistaking Sextus' avoidance of theory for an avoidance of belief altogether, puts forward the following false dilemma: either you must engage in the philosophical project of seeking the overall theory of everything, or you must retreat into your phenomenal shell. Unless you are willing to put forward your beliefs as we dogmatists do—as part of an overall theory of everything, stemming from incorrigible impressions, guaranteed by a criterion of *katalêpsis*, which you are willing to defend on demand—you cannot have any beliefs at all.

This distinction, between ordinary and everyday beliefs, is obviously much in need of elaboration. And when we look to Sextus for help, the passages in which he is most explicit about these issues suffer from a systematic ambiguity. According to the revisionist interpretation, these passages show that Sextus is trying to distinguish beliefs that are put forward as part of a big theory from ordinary beliefs. According to the radical interpretation, they show that Sextus is trying to distinguish all beliefs, beliefs of any kind, from comments about the sequence of mental images that play across his sensorium.

The reason for this systematic ambiguity is that the language of appearances, seeming, impressions, etc. can play many roles. The one that the rabid interpretation focuses on is its role in non-epistemic appearance claims. A typical case is the use of "seems" in the statement that the sun seems to move around the earth, when made by someone who fully believes that the sun does not move around the earth. It seems to, that is, but I believe that it really does not.

But there are other uses of the vocabulary of seeming. Sometimes, talk of seeming or appearance reflects an awareness that one's beliefs may not meet every possible standard of justification. When people say that something just seems a certain way to them, they are not always taking a detached attitude to the propositional content of that belief; they may believe it as vehemently as they believe anything at all. It may just reflect their awareness that they do not have any arguments for the position handy right now, or that they do not have any that will satisfy the person with whom they are speaking. When someone says that capital punishment just seems wrong to them, this phrase may express a very deep conviction; frequently the vocabulary of seeming makes its appearance after hours of argumentation have left both sides unconvinced. Despite all of the arguments that I have heard for capital punishment, some of which carry some weight; despite the fact that I have not presented my case against it very effectively, despite all of this, it just seems wrong to me. One can imagine someone talking this way; and expressing thereby anything but a detached, thin-blooded view of their belief. Someone talking this way may hold their conviction as strongly as anything else they believe; they may be willing to die for it (or execute their opponents). Saying that something seems to you a certain way is sometimes a way of marking one's own awareness that one cannot construct a complete justificatory account linking up the particular belief to cogent arguments based on premisses agreeable to all. But saying that it still seems to you that way, reflects the fact that you still believe it, despite your inability to articulate a justification for it.

One obvious case in which we cannot readily come up with a justification of the premise-conclusion sort is the case of sense-perception. If this book-cover seems green to me, as it does, then I do not believe that it is green as the result of an inference from some further things I believe. In fact, I would be at a loss to come up with anything like a set of premisses or a chain of deductions to try to support this belief. Nevertheless, I certainly do believe that it is green. If I were put in the room with Parmenides, who had very good arguments to show that there are no colors, or Anaxagoras, who had a not very good argument that snow is black, then there is a good chance that both of these people, who are vastly smarter than I am, would have the argumentative upper hand with me. They have everything on their side; dialectical brilliance, apparently undeniable premises, like "whatever is, is", and a much better command of Greek, too (as the old joke has it, the accomplishments of antiquity are due to the fact that the ancients got a good classical education). These thinkers are arch-dogmatists; they have an argument for everything, and they really believe that the outcome of argumentation has a status so privileged that it can override any other consideration. I, meanwhile, might be unable to produce a single good argument for my belief that the book is green. But after several hours, if I had not been converted to dogmatism, I would still believe that it was green. And I might well express this by saying, "Look, I am not very good at arguing about these things, but it just seems green to me. That is just how it seems."

And it would be a deep mistake to suppose that my assertion employs a non-epistemic appearance claim. For this is not like the case in which I say, e.g., "of course, I do not believe that the oar is bent, but it still seems bent." In the case of the book, I still believe that it is green; it seems green to me, and I believe it is green. My use of the language of appearance then marks no disinclination from belief. My exposure to the arguments against the book's being green has not affected my conviction about its color. It has merely shown me that I do not have arguments or evidence with which I can demonstrate its greenness to other people, e.g. to my disputants, and it is this which I mark with the language of appearance.[10]

Sense-perception, by its very nature, does not seem to come as the result of prior premisses or inferences. Accordingly, it forms an obvious paradigm of a belief whose origin is non-inferential. And I take it that this is a further reason why it is so often used by Sextus as an example of the sort of belief that the skeptic does have. But that doesn't mean that the Skeptic is committed only to sensory appearances. In trying to describe this sense of seeming, he just uses sense-perception as an illustration. Unfortunately, it too is an ambiguous one.

I have tried to indicate how I see the distinction between dog-

10. One might consider, in this regard, the poem of Evenus, the friend and contemporary of Socrates:

pollois antilegein men ethos peri pantos homoiôs,
orthôs d' antilegein, ouketi tout' en ethei.
kai pros men toutous arkei logos heis ho palaios
"soi men tauta dokount' estô, emoi de tade"
tous xunetous d' an tis peseie takhista legôn eu
hoiper kai rêistês eisi didaskaliês.

The use of "*dokeô*" in the fourth line has nothing of diffidence in it; it is a way of dismissing further debate, while retaining one's conviction.

matic and non-dogmatic belief manifested in some famous passages. But since their interpretation is still disputed, I shall not dwell on them any longer, but instead turn to some out-of-the-way passages that I think support the revisionist interpretation of the distinction. You can see Sextus making the distinction in the prefaces to many of his individual attacks on different subject areas. For instance, Sextus conducts an inquiry into philosophical theories of number, linguistics, astrology, and logic, and before each of them he makes it clear that his attack is only focused on the philosophical claims, not on the common or ordinary use of the things themselves. So, at the beginning of his attack on theoretical mathematics, he says.

> In the customary way we speak undogmatically of numbering a thing and understand that something is a number; but the extreme methods of the Dogmatists have provoked the attack upon numbers also. (PH III. 15 1)

With this he begins his scrutiny of the Pythagorean theory that everything is number, and so on. The distinction surely is something like the following: everyone counts things, and everyone believes there are numbers, and we use all of these things and would have trouble getting by without them. Of course, we do so with a fair degree of anomaly; we say both "there is a number between 3 and 5" and also "there is a number up there on the blackboard", and there may well be some confusion here. In the normal course of affairs this sort of anomaly never causes any trouble whatsoever. No more does it for the skeptic. In the normal course of events, no one doubts that if they have a large flock of sheep to count, there will be a number available to them that will be the number of that flock.

No more does the skeptic. But the dogmatists have gone so far beyond the uses of life, that they have made the notion of numbers unrecognizable. With their talk of Platonic form-numbers, and Pythagorean self-subsistent numbers, and so on, they have made a greater mess than they found; their *periergia* has led to more anomaly than was present hitherto. And that is all the skeptic attacks; he has no interest in challenging the schoolteacher's reminder that there is a number between 3 and 5, by claiming that numbers do not exist.

> For it is argued that if number exists, number is either the actual

> numerables or something else apart from them; but number is neither the actual numerables, as the Pythagoreans have proved, nor something else apart from them as we shall show; number, therefore, is nothing. (PH III.157)

The non-existence of number is the result of a dogmatic dilemma, each of whose limbs is closed off by further dogmatic arguments—Pythagorean arguments closing off one limb, Peripatetic arguments closing off the other. Why should this be at all convincing to someone who thinks that the dogmatists have just made trouble for themselves? It is obvious enough that there are numbers; we use them all the time. Can the average person justify that claim? No; but neither can the dogmatists. What will the average person say, if reduced to silence by some quick-witted Pythagorean? "Well, I may not be able to show you that numbers subsist or exist, if you mean something fancy by that, but it certainly seems to me that there are numbers, and that is what I go by:—how it seems to me." The skeptic's words precisely. Finishing his attack on dogmatical theories of number, Sextus concludes:

> But if number neither is conceived as self-existent, nor subsists in the numerables, then there is no such thing as number—to judge from the over-elaborations introduced by the Dogmatists (*hoson epi tais periergiais tais hupo tôn dogmatikôn eisenênegmenais*) (PH III.167)

The same distinction can be found in AM I, the discussion about grammar. Sextus makes it clear that he has no interest in challenging anyone's claim to know the alphabet, or in denying that letters, words, and so on all exist. What he designates for his target is technical grammar:

> However, since the art of Grammar is twofold—the one promising to teach the letters and their combinations and being in general an art of writing and reading, and the other being in comparison a more profound faculty and not consisting merely in the bare knowledge of letters but also in the investigation of their discovery and their nature, and in addition the parts of speech composed of letters and all other matters of the same kind—it is not our purpose now to controvert the former; for that it is useful is agreed by all men .... It might be thought by some that Timon is of the contrary opinion,...this however, does not appear

> to be the case .... What he means rather is this: "when a man has been taught the Punic symbols of Cadmus he need pay no attention to any further art of letters"; and this does not refer to the uselessness of the art which is found to deal with the letters and with employing them in writing and reading, but of that which is boastful and needlessly inquisitive .... Hence, while we not only have no fault to find with reading and writing, but even owe it the warmest thanks, we bring our critical weapons to bear on the rest of Technical Grammar. (AM I. 49-56)

More of the same can be found in the attack on "hellenism", or speaking Greek, an attack which again is explicitly limited in scope:

> There are two distinct kinds of "hellenism": one stands apart from our common usage and seems to proceed in accordance with linguistic theory; the other conforms to the common usage of each of the Greeks and is derived from framing words and from observation of ordinary conversation .... However, since there are two forms of "hellenism", we declare, for the reasons already stated, that the second is of great use, but the first useless for reasons which we shall now state (AM I. 176-177)

And with this he launches into his attack on "hellenism"; an attack only on the technical doctrine, not on correct speech in general. To those familiar with the ancient debate between "analogy" and "anomaly", it might seem obvious that Sextus would treat this pair as he treats any other set of conflicting systems, setting them in opposition and declaring the question irresolvable. Significantly, he does nothing of the sort; he consistently attacks analogical theories, and supports those accounts of language that give anomaly free rein. The reason for this, I take it, is that "anomaly" is not and never was the name of a system at all; those who resisted the analogists' hegemony were merely allowing language and its users to go their own way, without interference from pseudo-scientific theorizing about how languages ought to be. Championing *sunêtheia* is not setting up a new dogma, exactly because it is unruly, unpredictable, and admittedly arbitrary; usage varies not merely between languages or communities, but even within one speaker's idiolect, depending on his audience (AM I.228–235). This, I think, is an important model for Sextan skepticism in general; unfortunately the amount of material in AM I and II that bears upon it directly is so slim that no more than the suggestion can be made.

The discussion of Astrology (AM V) also begins by distinguishing useful reasons for looking at the sky from useless, dogmatical ones:

> [Our subject is not] the prediction practiced by Eudoxus and Hipparchus and men of their kind, which some also call to astronomy", for this, like [the study of the skies involved in] farming and piloting, consists in the observation of the phenomena (*têrêsis epi phainomenois*). It is rather "genethlialogy" (the study of the arrangement of stars on one's birthday), which the [astrologists] adorn with more high-sounding titles, describing themselves as "mathematicians" and "astrologers", treating ordinary folk with insolence in various ways, building a great bulwark of superstition against us, and allowing us to do nothing according to right reason.... The [astrologists], having too inquisitively (*periergoteron*) gazed up into the surrounding vault, declare.... (AM V.1-2)

One of the boasts of the philosophical schools was that they had technical methods for avoiding fallacies and resolving ambiguities—as now, this was a major component of the study of logic. Of course, their methods were far from perfect, and Sextus obliges them by pointing this out. At the end of his treatment of logic in the *Outlines* (PH II. 229-259), he concludes that the methods that the dogmatists (here primarily the Stoics) have developed for the resolution of these fallacies and ambiguities actually put them in worse shape than are the Skeptics, or anyone trained in a trade, or even a slave:

> Whereas we, by starting undogmatically (*adoxastôs*) from the observation of practical life, thus avoid these fallacious arguments, the Dogmatists will not be in a position to distinguish the Sophism from the argument which seems to be correctly propounded, seeing that they have to pronounce dogmatically that the form of the argument is, or is not, logically sound and also that the premisses are, or are not, true .... So in these sorts of cases the technical treatment of sophisms so much talked about amongst the Dialecticians is otiose.
>
> And we say much the same regarding the distinguishing of ambiguities. For ... all such ambiguities as can be usefully cleared

> up—such, that is, as occur in the course of some practical affair—will be cleared up, not certainly by the dialectician, but by the craftsmen trained in each several art, as they have personal experience of the conventional way adopted by themselves of using the terms to denote the objects signified .... And in the ordinary affairs of life we see already how people—even the slave-boys—distinguish ambiguities when they think such distinction is of use. Certainly, if a master has two servants with the same name, let's say "Manes", and he asked a slave-boy to go get Manes, the slave-boy will ask "Which one?" And if someone who had several different wines were to say to his boy "Pour me out a draught of wine," then too the boy will ask "Which one?" Thus it is the experience of what is useful in each affair that brings about the distinguishing of ambiguities.
>
> All such ambiguities, however, as are not involved in the practical experiences of life but in dogmatic opinions, and are no doubt useless for a life void of dogmatism—concerning these the Dialectician, in his own peculiar position will be similarly forced, in view of the Skeptical attacks, to suspend judgment, in so far as they are probably linked up with matters that are non-evident and non-apprehensible, or even non-substantial. (PH II.254-258)

Sextus' comments here show that the distinction between dogma and the non-dogmatic is not some distinction between the external world and the solipsistic internal realm of non-epistemic appearances, but rather the distinction between technical methods that make elevated claims to generality, insight or infallibility, as opposed to informal methods followed in common life.

The Stoics claim to have a method for resolving ambiguities and avoiding fallacies. It is admirably systematic and non-ad hoc; it stems from their general theory of language and logic. This, in turn, has organic roots in their metaphysical theories of, e.g., the ontological status of the *lekton* or sayable. And yet with all of this formidable machinery ready to be wheeled up to the breach, they still cannot solve many fallacies—some of which would never arise outside of the context of their theories (this is what Sextus has been expounding since PH II.229). Not only have they not been able to overcome the anomaly in things, they actually have produced a system with novel anomalies of its own.

Meanwhile, ordinary life has arrived at ways of resolving many of the ambiguities to which ordinary life gives rise. Not all of them, perhaps; there is still much anomaly in things. But when the slave-boy is given an ambiguous order, he doesn't need to consult Chrysippus in order to find out how to disambiguate it. He doesn't have a theory about language (much less a metaphysics to ground it in), and he does not have a general method for resolving any and every ambiguity. But neither is he frozen into immobility by his lack of philosophical training. He just does what seems right, or what anyone would do, or what strikes him as the thing to do right then.

And again, as with the school-child's assent, it should seem implausible that the slave-boy is engaged in any elaborate epistemic artifice, whereby he seems to be talking about other servants or containers of wine, but is in fact only carrying on a monologue about his internal appearances. He presumably believes that there are these two other servants, and a selection of wines, even though these beliefs cannot be a matter of his "noting how things appear to him" (in Burnyeat's phrase); indeed, the absent servants presumably do not appear to him in any way at the time he is asking his master to specify the one he wants.

This entire repertoire of belief content is distinguished from the "dogmatic opinions … concerning which the dogmatist too [viz. along with the Skeptic] will be forced to suspend judgment, in so far as they are probably linked up with matters that are non-evident and nonapprehensible, or even non-substantial". To the extent that this shows us where Sextus himself wants to draw the distinction, it shows us that the traditional view cannot be right.

A few points of interest can be derived from these and other passages. One is that there are certain phrases and characterizations that tend to appear in the passages where Sextus is distinguishing the dogmatic from the non-dogmatic. Among these are terms that mean roughly "make-work" or "meddler" (*periergos*); the dogmatist is not merely a busybody, but a bungler who makes things worse by his exertions. Equally common are terms meaning "endless argumentation" (*apeirologia*), "the hunting up of arguments" (*heurêsilogia*), and so on. Given that this is how he characterizes the dogmatists, the skeptic cannot possibly be ranging himself against the grocer, the farmer, and the parent. The figure of the dogmatist in Sextus is characterized by a handful of epithets, generally derogatory, which apply quite handily to professional pedants, speculative scientists, and the members of the ancient schools, but bear little resemblance to the ordinary possessor of ordinary beliefs.[11]

The discussion of the two kinds of grammar also gives us good evidence about the kind of claims to scientific status that trigger the skeptic's enquiry. Crafts in general, after all, do not come in for skeptical scrutiny; it is only when they arrogate to themselves a status like that of philosophy, either in their methods or results, or when, as with Chaldaean astronomy, they begin to "treat ordinary folk with insolence in various ways", that the skeptic responds. We can see grammatistic trying to borrow respectability both from medicine (a paradigmatic ancient art) and geometry (surely the paradigmatic ancient science) by arguing that they too overcame the humble origins implicit in their names:

> ... for just as *iatrikê* was so named in olden times from the extraction of *ioi*, but is now applied to the curative treatment of all other ailments as well, which is a much higher form of art (*technikôterê*); and just as geometry derived its name originally from the mensuration of land, but is at present applied also to theory concerned with more fundamental entities (*hê tôn phusikôterôn theôria*), so also the perfected art of letters (*hê teleios grammatikê*), after being named originally from the knowledge of letters, was extended so as to comprise acquaintance with the more complex and technical theories (*technikôtera theôrêmata*) about them. (AM I.45-46)

It is the claim to technicality that Sextus disputes; accordingly

11. Burnyeat 1984 attempts to refute the revisionist interpretation by showing that a distinction between ordinary and philosophical beliefs cannot be found in Sextus' discussions of place at AM X.15 and PH III.119. It is true, that the distinction Burnyeat finds there (between *topos pros akribeian and topos en platei*) is not the distinction that the skeptic makes between the appearances he abolishes and those he does not, between the *dogmata* he has and those he does not, and so on. It is a different distinction, one that clearly originates in certain dogmatical arguments for the possibility of motion, against the Zenonian and Diodorean arguments that motion is impossible. Sextus himself never uses those two phrases to mark the ordinary/philosophical distinction elsewhere, and in fact only re-uses the phrases in one other context (AM V.88), a dispute about astrology, indirectly connected with time (which presumably inspired the title of Burnyeat's article, although he does not discuss it). The distinction between *topos pros akribeian* and *topos en platei* has no particular connection to any distinction between philosophical and everyday beliefs; but then it is not clear why Burnyeat thought it might, or why he thought the passages decisive one way or another. Another mark of the irrelevance of these passages is the absence in them of any of the typical terms (*periergia* etc.) just mentioned.

an admission that the discipline is untechnical is sufficient to call off the skeptical attack:

> Moreover, since the majority of them have agreed that [the historical part of grammatistic] is non-technical and consists of unmethodical matter (*atechnon kai ek tês amethodou hulês*), they have relieved us from having to argue further against them (*apolelukasi men hêmas tês epi pleion pros autous antirrêseôs*) (AM I.254)

Music comes in for scrutiny because of its claims to produce results like those of philosophy:

> If, [the musicians] say, we welcome philosophy as regulating human life and repressing the passions of the soul, much more shall we welcome Music, because it produces the same results as philosophy… (AM VI.7)

I hope that a consideration of Sextus' attitude towards reading, writing, counting and music will show what is meant in the following quote:

> For it is, I think, sufficient to conduct one's life empirically and undogmatically in accordance with the rules and beliefs that are commonly accepted, suspending judgment regarding the statements derived from dogmatic subtlety and furthest removed from the usage of life. (PH II.246)

He only suspends judgment about the abstruse and technical pronouncements of the professional philosophers; for the rest, he lives just as anyone else does. Here again, the perennial charge of masquerading will raise its head; the skeptic lives "according to" commonly accepted beliefs, but he doesn't *really* believe them, he only pretends to. But what does this mean? The ordinary person really believes that if you put water over a fire it will boil; what in the above quote prevents the Skeptic from believing the same? What the Skeptic does not take a stand on is whether water is the true substance of everything, as Thales thought, or instead is transmuted into air by having its form-triangles resolved as Plato thought. That is the dogmatic subtlety he avoids; nothing else.

Consequently, the revisionist interpretation supposes that Sextus has lots of beliefs, about all sorts of matters. Take anyone that you meet on the street (any non-philosopher), and consider what sorts of things they believe and indeed know; all of these things are open to the skeptic. What the average person will not have is a systematic account of how all of these beliefs fit together, a demonstration that all of them are consistent, an axiomatization of the entire set showing which are deduced from which, and arguments that all of the axioms are indubitable and irrefutable. Nor does the skeptic; and nor, in the skeptic's experience, do any of the dogmatical schools. But this is exactly the kind of system that they claim to have; and that is why the skeptic's employment of arguments takes the forms that it does. The skeptic employs the modes of circularity, regress, and so on, precisely because the dogmatists claim to have fully worked out, foundationally justified theories of everything. Accordingly, the best characterization of a dogmatic belief is that it is a belief put forward as though it were part of such a theory.

The skeptic's investigations are thus directed only at such beliefs, and the form that they take is that of pointing out to the dogmatists that their beliefs fail on the very terms on which they are put forward. That is, they fail according to the criteria that the dogmatists think are the criteria for something being part of the theory of everything. But of course, part of such a theory will be a theory about criteria as well;[12] and in refraining from endorsing any of the dogmatists' theories, the skeptic also refrains from endorsing their theories about what are the right criteria for belief, too. The skeptic might not believe something even if it met the dogmatists' criteria; or he might believe things that do not meet their criteria. The skeptic will presumably not have any general rule about what things he can believe or not; criteria of that kind are among the things he is still searching for.

Meanwhile, he just follows how things seem to him.

12. The point is made in Frede 1979.

Chapter Five

Details of Sextus' Ethics

The skepticism found in Sextus Empiricus' writings is not generally thought to have an ethical component in the way that, e.g., Stoicism does; and this for several reasons. For, first of all, the *Outlines* and the books *Against the Professors* contain relatively few descriptions of virtue and vice, moral exempla, or discussions about the requirements of ethical conduct; Sextus does not read like Seneca. Secondly, the one tenet of Skepticism that might be taken as an injunction about how one ought to live, namely that one should suspend belief, has been taken primarily as an epistemological, rather than an ethical tenet. And its predicted effects on the conduct of life are studied, not for themselves, but for their epistemological consequences. That is to say, that students of skepticism have started from the premiss that an epistemological theory must be responsive to certain practical requirements of daily maintenance, and then attacked Skepticism by trying to show that it is inadequate to these practical requirements. So even this critical strategy was aimed at Skepticism's alleged consequences for epistemology, not ethics. Thirdly, if Skepticism was thought to advocate the suspension of belief as a principle about how one ought to live one's life, this was held to be itself an inconsistency within the system, assent to the proposition that nothing should be assented to. But the failure was still felt to be local to the epistemology, and in some sense predictable; the same charge of self-refutation has even been made against Socrates' professions of ignorance. It was not seen as part of any larger theory that the Skeptic might have about his own actions and their ends; indeed, the fact that the Skeptic even claims to have an end is given short shrift in most discussions of Skepticism. A good example of this sort of instrumental interest in the ethical content of skepticism can be seen in Annas and Barnes' introduction to their edition of *The Modes of Skepticism.*[1] There, they use the character of the *ataraxia* that skepticism promised as an means of inferring the sort of beliefs that skepticism attacked:

> "The doubt [the skeptics] expected to induce was ordinary, non-philosophical doubt; it excluded beliefs, and it was therefore a practical doubt. Indeed, it was precisely by reference to the practical corollaries of their doubt that they used to recommend their philosophy: scepticism, they claimed, by relieving us of our ordinary beliefs, would remove the worry from our lives and ensure our happiness."

If Sextus left our ordinary beliefs intact, the argument goes, he could not rid us of our ordinary concerns. So he must have targeted all beliefs, not just philosophical ones. But the argument fails, for Sextus never claims to rid us of our ordinary concerns. The skeptic's end, after all, is not merely tranquillity; it is tranquillity in respect of *dogmata* (i.e. so far as anxiety induced by philosophical belief goes), and moderate affections in everything else. Skepticism cannot rid us of ordinary worries and sufferings; but it can still perform an extraordinary service for Dogmatists. And it is Dogmatists who are the skeptic's target audience, as PH III.280 makes clear. For they have additional disturbances and worries that no-one would have, who did not subscribe to one of the schools. They are disturbed when they do not have the things that their schools describe as good, and irrationally elated when they have them.[2]

We can read about the self-induced disturbances of the dogmatists all throughout the pages of antiquity. For instance, there was the Pythagorean who bit out her own tongue, rather than vio-

1. Annas and Barnes 1985.
2. PH I.30, PH III.235-238, AM XI.116-118. It is a deep and enduring problem for my interpretation that, whereas the second two passages clearly refer to Dogmatists suffering from beliefs about things good and bad by nature, the first passage refers to "*idiôtai*", which is most naturally translated "non- specialists". Unless we take the desperate measure of understanding this as "non-Skeptical philosophers", there is the obvious implication that the Skeptic is here distinguishing himself from nonphilosophers as well as Dogmatic philosophers, and advocating a revision of non-philosophical beliefs about good and evil.

late the school's prohibition against eating legumes.[3] There was Philetas of Kos, who drove himself to death because he could not solve the liar paradox.[4] There was the dialectician who killed himself because he could not resolve a sophistical puzzle.[5] There were the Cyrenaics, persuaded to kill themselves by Hegesias, until the local authorities closed his school as a health hazard.[6] There was Kleombrotus the Ambraciot, who read Plato's Phaedo and threw himself off a wall to his death.[7] Cratylus the Heracleitian was so troubled by flux that he eventually reduced himself to speechlessness.[8] These disturbances do not stem from ordinary beliefs; many of us who are worried about how to pay the bills are not yet suicidal about Russell's antinomy.

Then so far as irrational elation goes, one need only consider the state of the proper Stoic who watches his children being tortured with a feeling of tranquil joy at the progress of the cosmos,[9] or the state of the Epicurean who instead of feeling pained at the death of a close friend, delights in the reflection that he can always find other friends just as hedonically useful—indeed, that if all of his friends and family were to be killed, he could still find a ready supply of the good things that nature provides. The good Epicurean, the Epicurean who lives according to the doctrines of his school, will be found at his spouse's deathbed without a tear in his eye, filled with the deepest joy and contentment when he contemplates how readily he can find his heart's content in a little pot of cheese.[10] Our natural reaction, that such a person is deeply disturbed, is voiced by Sextus at PH I.27 when he says that the dogmatists are immoderately and irrationally elated when they have what their philosophical theories tell them are good. The adherents of the schools suffer these irrational agonies and irrational elations only because of their adherence to the dogmata of their school; and it is only those agonies and elations that Sextus offers to relieve. You would never have this sort of anxiety or hysterical glee unless

3. Olympiodorus in Phaedonem—I thank Prof. Richard Sorabji for bringing this passage to my attention.
4. Athenaeus, *Deipnosophistae* 401c
5. Diogenes Laertius II.112
6. Cicero, Disp. Tusc. 1.34,84
7. AM I.48
8. Ar. *Meta*. 1010a12
9. On this now see Brennan 1998b.
10. Diogenes Laertius X.11=Usener fr. 182

you were committed to a whole superstructure of theoretical beliefs—normal people, people who are neither insane nor adherents of a philosophical sect, neither kill themselves if they cannot analyze arguments, nor sit through funerals giggling over dairy products. This may sound like caricature, but it is not; it is simply a sampling of ancient philosophical doctrine. And seeing what it means to live according to philosophical doctrine, gives us greater insight into why Sextus says in AM XI.165 that his not having any philosophical beliefs does not prevent him from living, but merely means that he lives as others do, instead of living in accordance with philosophical arguments. It is not that he does not study philosophical arguments, or that he thinks them unimportant or doomed to futility; indeed, to be a skeptic just means to be engaged in the ongoing search for truth according to philosophy. But this ongoing search for the truth according to philosophy is combined with a commitment to ordinary life and ordinary beliefs. In this regard, we may reconsider Burnyeat's description of the state of affective anaesthesia with which he threatens the skeptic:

> If a tyrant sends a message that you and your family are to perish at dawn unless you commit some unspeakable deed, the true skeptic will be undisturbed both about whether the message is true or false and about whether it would be a good thing or a bad thing to comply with the command. You will be undisturbed ... because you have been rendered unable to find any reason to think anything is true rather than false or good rather than bad .... That is ataraxia .... The life without belief is not an achievement of the will but a paralysis of reason itself.[11]

If one considers the theorems of Stoic ethics, it should be clear that this is a much better description of the Sage than of the Skeptic. For although it is true that the Sage does think that there is a good (acting wisely or virtuously) and a bad (acting foolishly or viciously), still he does not think that these notions can be given any substantive content; there is no act, normally so described, that is in itself a good act; nor any that is bad. The only act, if one can so call it, that is always incumbent upon us has the trivial description: living virtuously.[12] Everything else—telling the truth

11. Burnyeat 1980a
12. On this now see Brennan 1996

or lying, honoring one's parents or eating them, serving one's state or betraying it, all of these may be virtuous or vicious alike, depending on circumstance. If it is part of the divine logos that one should obey the tyrant and slaughter innocents, then the virtuous thing to do is willingly to obey and willingly to slaughter, without the faintest touch of unease. In fact, to feel any repugnance, to feel anything but the calm *khara* of harmonious life, would be to act viciously indeed. Or if Zeus and *Peprômenê* have so ordained that you should refuse the tyrant's command, then your family goes to it; they are not near your conscience. Not only should you not be troubled by their deaths, you should feel genuinely elated; you are as happy as it is possible to be. So long as your logos is in harmony with the divine logos, so long as you are acting rationally and consistently and are untouched by any false beliefs, then there is no one happier than you; you may truly be compared to the gods themselves in their blessedness. On the other hand, if you were to resist or doubt in any way, then you would have lost the sum of your bliss; now, having become bad and vicious in an instant, you would be as miserable as someone on the rack. The loss of your family would still be inconsequential, of course; but the loss of your wisdom would mean that there was no one more wretched, no one more unhappy than you. That is not a caricature of the Stoic view; it is the Stoic view.

> For the one who dogmatizes that something is good or bad by nature suffers from disturbances continuously. When the things that seem good to him are not present, he thinks he is being tortured by the things that are bad by nature, and he then pursues what he believes to be the good. And when he has obtained this he falls into further disturbances, through his irrational and immoderate elation, and fearing the reversal he will do anything in order not to lose the things that appear good to him. (PH I.27)

Of course, the Skeptic's attitude toward this sort of case must itself be rather complicated. On the one hand, that only reason is good and only folly bad is surely not part of the ordinary view. And reflecting on these Stoic claims has not produced any inclination to belief in the Skeptic; they have left him entirely unpersuaded. But, at the same time, ethics is a very complicated subject that is not yet fully sorted out, and the Skeptic is committed to the continuing search for truth according to philosophy—that is what characterizes the Skeptical school as a whole (PH I.1-4). Perhaps further searching will lead to the conviction that the Stoics are right after all; at any rate, none of the arguments against the Stoic view have persuaded the Skeptic of its negation, either; he is neither persuaded nor dissuaded, but feels an equal lack of both persuasion and dissuasion (*isotês kata pistin kai apistian*—PH I. 10). What is clear, however, is that the Stoic position is not one that should be adopted lightly or without consideration. Before one decides that one's family's fate is inconsequential, and that the tyrant's unspeakable acts are not really bad after all, one should have some very weighty reasons. One ought to have some compelling motivation, be it in the form of arguments, evidence or whatever, before one overturns so much of ordinary life. And this, the Stoics surely do not have, even on their own criteria. After extensive consideration of both sides of the matter, the Skeptic does not feel that the Stoics have produced a compelling case. Of course, the Skeptic is also aware of his own fallibility in studying and assessing arguments, and of the possibility that more and better proofs will be forthcoming. He is not refuting the Stoics in the way an Epicurean would, so as to erect a new dogma in their place. That is why he contents himself with saying, not that the Stoic arguments are inadequate, but that he *feels* them to be inadequate; they produce no compelling persuasion in him, and he merely describes his own reaction to them ("in the utterance of the *phônai* (e.g. "No more", or I do not cognize") he states what appears to himself, and announces his own impression in an undogmatic way" PH I.15). And even this reaction can only be a reaction to the arguments he has encountered so far; that is why his *phônai* are all statements of how things appear to him now, which record the state of the debate at the moment ("*kata to nun phainomenon hêmin historikôs apangellomen peri hekastou*" PH I.4). The skeptics themselves will continue to seek truth until it is found; the dogmatists may someday do better. Their rashness consists just in their willingness to throw away so much of what ordinary life consists in, for such light and insubstantial reasons as they have now.

So much by way of clarifying what the Skeptic means by saying that his end is tranquillity in respect to matters of dogma. But one might still have interpretive qualms about how the Skeptic can have any positive views about the end at all. For, as I will argue, the Skeptic does proclaim an end, and proclaims it as an end, in the same way as other ethical theories do. It was a commonplace of Hellenistic thinkers, that the final end is, in the formulation of Aristotle's EN I.ii, that which is done for its own sake, while everything else is done for the sake of it—it was such a commonplace, indeed, that the Skeptic too endorses it. But it seems to me that the Skeptic cannot adopt this definition without adding to it a great deal of explanation, because of the sense in which he says he is a Skeptic. For, according to Sextus a Skeptic is not, at root, someone who eschews all beliefs, or argues on both sides, or any of the other characterizations that we normally associate with the name. Rather a skeptic is one who is seeking. And in particular, a Skeptic, as a member of one of the three greatest genera of philosophers, is seeking the truth. But this makes the Skeptic's profession of an end, and his adoption of the standard concept of a final end, problematic, exactly because of the relation between truth and the tranquillity which is his end. What the Skeptic has to show us is that 1) he really is pursuing truth; 2) that its attainment really is not necessary for the attainment of tranquillity; and 3) that his pursuit of the truth is still "for the sake of" tranquillity, in the way spelled out in the definition.

If the Skeptic cannot show us that he really is, in a satisfying sense, still pursuing the truth, then he falls into the camp of the Academic or Dogmatic Skeptics. He needs to show the second point, as well, in order to show us that tranquillity and suspension really are consistent. And he needs to show us the third point, because he endorses the formal definition of the end and so presumably thought that the rest of his system consistent with it.

Of these three problems, the first two are generally recognized. In particular, 1) and 2) capture much of the traditional allegations against the Skeptic, that he is not really continuing to search but has actually ended his enquiry with the (self-refuting) belief that one ought to believe nothing; and that genuine suspension would lead not to tranquillity but to abject misery. The third problem, however, has not, so far as I can tell, been considered. The reason why I think it is a problem, and why I think it is a different and worrying problem from those raised above, is as follows; it seems to me that the Skeptic can defend himself from the criticisms of 1) and 2) above, and show that his system is not internally incoherent on those issues. In the preceding chapters I have already tried to show how he might conduct that defense. But the way in which he does this may make it impossible for him still to endorse the definition of the end as "that for the sake of which all else". To put this third problem in summary form, if attaining truth really is not necessary for tranquillity, then how can the Skeptic say that he pursues the truth *for the sake* of the tranquillity?

In considering the Skeptics, it is important first to see that they do profess a final end, and that they endorse the traditional definition of the final end as that for the sake of which all else is done. Then we should convince ourselves that the Skeptic really does claim to be pursuing truth. Only when we see both of these things can we see why the relation between these points is worth investigating.

It may strike the reader as surprising that the Skeptic has a view about the end at all. One imagines, naturally enough, that whatever the Skeptic might have to say about ends would be wholly negative and critical, deriding the inconsistencies of the dogmatists in positing so many and such varied ends, and arguing that the end does not exist, and that even if it did it could not be taught, and so on.

Two surprises thus go hand in hand. For, first of all, the Skeptic does have an end, which Sextus tells us about it in the twelfth section of the *Outlines*. He both tells us what an end is in general, and what the Skeptic's end is. And his general formula for an end is fundamentally the same as that endorsed by the other schools,[13] but also adds an interesting further qualification: "Now a telos is that for the sake of which all action and contemplation are undertaken,[14] while it is done for the sake of nothing; or the ultimate object of desires. And we say still that the Skeptic's end is tranquillity in respect of matters of opinion, and moderate affection in matters of compulsion."[15] And in telling us what an end is in general, and what the Skeptic's end is in particular, he employs none of the usual Skeptical tags that we expect, such as "perhaps" or "it seems", or "but this is said undogmatically"; there is something unexpectedly positive about this chapter.[16]

The second surprise follows on this one, when we look either at Sextus' book *Against the Ethicists* (AM XI) or at the section of the

13. See, for the Stoics e.g., SVF 111.2; for the Epicureans e.g. de Finibus 1.29

14. This is Bury's translation for the literal "everything is done or contemplated"; the departure from the Greek seems justified. It might sound as though what is contemplated is the desirability or feasibility of doing something

15. *esti men oun telos to hou kharin panta prattetai ê theôreitai, auto de oudenos heneka; ê to eskhaton tôn orektôn. phamen de achri nun telos einai tou skeptikou tên en tois kata doxan ataraxian kai en tois katênagkasmenois metriopatheian*. PH I.12

16. Although, naturally, not too much weight can be put upon their local absence, since Sextus is so careful to tell us at the beginning of the *Outlines* that all of its contents are covered by a blanket qualifier.

Outlines that summarizes it (PH III 168-279). For neither of these contains, anywhere, a critical discussion of the final end. They neither contain discussions of the general concept of an end, nor criticisms of the dogmatists' particular candidate ends. This second must be qualified, but in a way that supports the overall point quite strikingly. That is, Sextus does have a variety of arguments against Epicurus' espousal of pleasure, or the Stoics' espousal of virtue and wisdom, and these are, in fact, their respective ends. But Sextus does not criticize them *as* ends, or even call them ends.[17] His entire argument is developed around the notion of a good or bad by nature, and when he attacks, e.g., pleasure, it will be in terms of pleasure's being put forward as the good by nature. The natural good and evil, not the end as such, is everywhere the object of his enquiry. And he makes this his conscious principle, at the beginning of the longer discussion, saying "But since almost all [the Dogmatists] have assumed, in agreement with one another, that ethical theory arises in connection with the distinction between goods and evils ... we too shall have to begin by enquiring into the difference."

When one considers that Aristotle's ethics takes as its first and fundamental notion that of an end, and that to Cicero it seemed obvious that the central topic of ethics, and the one from which all other distinctions between schools ultimately flowed, was that of the final end, it must seem rather disingenuous on Sextus' part to talk as though all of the dogmatists begin their ethical theorizing with the natural good and bad.[18] Nevertheless, the topic of ends in general, the fact that what he attacks as natural goods were also considered ends, the very fact that it was another commonplace of ethics that the end just is the natural good and vice versa, none of these issues is discussed anywhere in Sextus' discussions of ethics.

It seems that Sextus is consciously distinguishing between ends and natural goods, and subjecting the second to his normal Skeptical scrutiny, while sparing the first. This is evident as well in his procedure in PH I.12. For no sooner has he told us what an end is, and what the Skeptic's end is, than he tells us that who ever has

17. There is only one point in A.M. XI at which Sextus uses the word *telos* to refer to a dogmatist's end (Epicurean pleasure); otherwise he uses it either of the Skeptic's end (twice) or in a non-ethical sense (once).

18. EN I.1 et passim; Cicero de Finibus (i.e. "On Ends") passim, and esp. dF IV.14, V.15: "...he is especially eager to hear about the summum bonum, since once this is established, everything in philosophy is established" (audire de summo bono potissimum velit; hoc enim constituto in philosophia constituta sunt omnia).

an opinion about the good and bad by nature must be constantly disturbed. If his own statements about the end constituted opinions about the naturally good and bad, then they would be radically self-defeating; by opining that tranquillity was the good, he would rule out the possibility of his attaining tranquillity. Now it could be that he thinks his statements do not constitute a case of opining; that would be sufficient to get him out of the trap. And indeed, I think that we may come to decide that his view about the end is not an instance of the kind of dogma he condemns. But I hope the references to the specifically ethical discussions will convince the reader that Sextus is also denying the equivalence between the final end and the natural good, and that that is at least part of why he does not feel threatened by his condemnation of those who have opinions about a natural good.

So in some sense he does hold that an end is that for the sake of which everything is done, while it is done for nothing else; and that his end is in fact tranquillity; and he never questions either his conception of the end, or the concept of ends generally. It will be important later on to see how he might hold this belief or view, how he might have come to hold it, and how he might now justify holding it if he wished to. But it seems important first simply to note that he does, and that his doing so is reflected both in particular arguments and in his overall treatment of ethics.

Having seen that the Skeptic has a declared end, and that this is tranquillity, we should next verify that the Skeptic claims to be pursuing truth. It is worth emphasizing that this is Sextus' claim, in the first chapter of the *Outlines*. He first makes a very general claim about people seeking any object—e.g., some food to eat. The claim is that one of three things will happen: they will either find it, or decide that it is unfindable, or continue searching. This is equivalent to saying that, having started, they will continue searching until they have found it or decided that it cannot be found.

Sextus then takes as an instance of this general principal one particular search, whose object he characterizes in two ways. He says that "in the case of the things sought according to philosophy, some have claimed to have found the truth (while others, etc.)" (*epi tôn kata philosophian zêtoumenôn hoi men heurekenai to alêthes ephasan* …). It seems that the object of this particular search can be described in two ways, either as "those things sought according to philosophy", or as "the truth".

It is this object, whether described as the truth or as what is sought according to philosophy, that the Skeptic claims still to be searching for. And, according to his principle of trichotomy, the only way that the search can end is either by his claiming to have found the object, or by his claiming that the object cannot be found. One would like to know more about the force of this principle. For instance, it could be made to look analytic, if we assumed that the termination of a search before the object had been found would simply be taken as a denial that it could be found. But this would then make the general claim less plausible. For one could begin searching for food, and later stop searching, neither because one had found it nor because one had decided it could not be found, but because, e.g., one's fatigue or thirst had come to take precedence over one's need for food, so that one either stopped searching by falling asleep or by beginning a new search for water. Of course, this could be interpreted as constituting a denial that the food could be found, under some very weak and circumstantial notion of necessity, e.g., I cannot find food given my fatigue, or without suffering great thirst, or something of the sort. But it does not otherwise seem that breaking off a search without finding the object entails any belief that the object cannot be found—one might simply cease to consider the object worth searching for. Nevertheless, by denying that he has found his object, and by denying that the object cannot be found, the Skeptic claims still to be searching for the truth, or for the things sought in accordance with philosophy.

The apparent extensional equivalence of these two descriptions of the object of search lends further support to our overall position, that the Skeptic does have opinions about some things. For the presence of two characterizations of the object suggests that the truth that the Skeptic denies having is not any and every truth, but the truth about things sought after in accordance with philosophy.[19] This might often be a distinction of subject matter;

19. I am not careful to distinguish, in what follows, between two readings of "*tôn kata philosophian zêtoumenôn*". One reading would take it to refer to true beliefs or propositions; what we seek according to philosophy is the true account of, e.g., the sun, or the valid conditional. In this sense, "the things sought according to philosophy" would be identical to "the truth"; i.e., individual true beliefs, adding up to the true picture of everything. Another reading would take it as "the objects investigated or inquired into according to philosophy"; i.e., the things that we want to know about, like the sun, or the valid conditional, which form the subject-matter of the truths. In that case, the truth would not be equivalent to *tôn zêtoumenôn* but rather would be the truth *about tôn zêtoumenôn*. I speak in both ways, but I do not think there is anything vicious about doing so.

that is, the Skeptic will believe that there is a car coming toward him, but not that everything is or is not atoms and void. But as Frede himself notes, "matters are presumably more complicated .... [E]verything, if considered only as an object for reason, can be called into question .... Nothing, looked at in this way, will be evident to the Skeptic ...."[20] Frede's point, that the distinction between dogmatic beliefs and non-dogmatic beliefs is rather one of approach than subject matter, seems to be well captured by Sextus' use of the prepositional phrase; it is objects sought *according to philosophy* that the Skeptic searches for, and it is beliefs about objects *as objects of philosophy* that the Skeptic does not have. There may be theories about what the sun is, or what heat is, but when the Skeptic says that the sun is hot today, he is not doing it as a part of any of these theories. The sun may sometimes be an object of philosophical enquiry, and truths about it may be sought according to philosophy, but when the Skeptic opines about it he does not opine about it according to philosophy. So his possession of opinions about some matter does not conflict with his claim not to have opinions, because it is opinions of a certain type, opinions held in a certain way, namely as philosophical opinions, that he denies having.

Conversely, it is opinions about objects *as* objects of philosophical enquiry that the Skeptic (or better the proto-Skeptic) began searching for, in common with his Dogmatic colleagues, and thus it must be beliefs of that kind that he is still be searching for. Presumably it would be very misleading for Sextus to say that he is still searching, if he had stopped searching for one thing and began searching for some other thing. His claim to engaged in an ongoing search, if this is to distinguish him from the Academic, must mean that he is still seeking the things sought in accordance with philosophy, in the same way in which he began. And in order for the Skeptic still to be seeking the things sought in accordance with philosophy, he must still believe that it is a real possibility that the object of this search—truth of the kind specified—be attained. The search that gives the Skeptic his name is not the search for equipollent arguments, or the search for tranquillity, or the search for a cure for rashness or self conceit. That is the claim that Sextus puts forward in the first chapter.

I think it important to bring out these two facts, that the Skeptic claims that his end is tranquillity, and that the Skeptic claims still to

20. Frede 1979 p. 195.

be seeking truth. On the other hand, the view that I have set myself to challenge takes it that what the Skeptic claims is relatively uninteresting, because, on their picture, the Skeptic is systematically disingenuous in any case. Regardless of what he claims to be doing, the Skeptic must be a closet dogmatist of one kind or another; and his claims are either intentionally misleading or merely self-deluded, perhaps the result of failure to pay attention to his own actual practice. We have seen this same critical disagreement in Chapter 2 with the matter of the criterion, and once again I shall construct my exposition as a response to Burnyeat's position.

Burnyeat argues that the Skeptics have two problems, one on either side, as it were, of *epokhê*.[21] The Skeptic's state of *epokhê* is preceded, as PH I.iv tells us, by the opposing of argument and appearance to one another; that is, by the Skeptic's characteristic and habitual activity, stemming from his skeptical "*dunamis antithetikê*". The Skeptic's state of *epokhê* is followed, "as a shadow follows a body", by tranquillity. So the progression, as we are told at several places, is from equality of opposed positions, to *epokhê* , to *ataraxia*.

Between three stages there are two steps, and each of these, in Burnyeat's opinion, is a mis-step for the Skeptic. Moving from the equality of opposed positions to *epokhê*, Burnyeat claims, is coming to hold a belief of exactly the type that the Skeptics disavow: "[A]ccepting the conclusion that p on the basis of a certain argument is hardly to be distinguished from coming to *believe* that p is true with that argument as one's reason."[22] The Skeptic accepts the conclusion that every dogmatic claim has a contrary equally worth or unworthy of acceptance; that is the p of interest in the above quote.[23] And he accepts this conclusion as the result of a great deal of meticulous and painstaking argumentation. So this conclusion, the formula of his *epokhê*, is a belief, based on reasons. Thus the Skeptic's first mis-step, on Burnyeat's analysis.

Then in moving from *epokhê* to tranquillity, the Skeptic falters again. His *epokhê* is expressed by such formulations as "there are equal arguments for and against this conclusion", or "I determine nothing", or "no more this than that". "But," says Burnyeat, "this

21. Burnyeat 1980a.
22. Burnyeat 1980a p. 50, all emphasis in original.
23. I say that this is the p of interest only in that this is the particular belief to which Burnyeat wants to apply his general claim. In the quote, Burnyeat is making a claim of perfectly general application; he thinks this is true of any p.

should not mean he is left in a state of actually wondering whether p or not-p is the case, for that might induce anxiety. Still less should he be wondering whether, in general, contrary claims are equally balanced. For if it is a real possibility for him that they are not, that means it is a real possibility that there are answers to be found; and it will be an immense worry to him, as it was at the very beginning of his skeptical education, that he does not know what these answers are." If *epokhê* really does lead to tranquillity, it must be an *epokhê* in which the Skeptic is "satisfied ... that contrary claims are indeed equal". And the only sort of satisfaction sufficient for forestalling this anxiety is one that involves belief. So once again, Burnyeat concludes, in order for the Skeptic to take the step from *epokhê* to *ataraxia*, he must have beliefs of the sort that he explicitly disavows. And these beliefs must render purely pro forma the Skeptic's claim still to be engaged in an ongoing enquiry; Burnyeat denies that the Skeptic has "an active programme of research."

Burnyeat could have elaborated on the second charge in an even more damaging fashion; his decision not to stems, I assume, from *philanthropia*. Burnyeat could have accused the Pyrrhonian not merely of having a belief, but of being a covert Academic, dogmatic Skeptic. Instead, he grants Sextus' wish to differentiate himself from that tribe: the Skeptic is a covert believer, but he "...is not a negative dogmatist furnished with a priori objections that rule out the possibility of answers as a matter of general principle once and for all." But certainly this is puzzling, given what Burnyeat has argued so far. If a negative dogmatist, in Sextus' opening tripartition, were one who had "a priori" reasons, then perhaps Burnyeat's charge of belief would not be the same as a charge of dogmatic skepticism. But, for obvious reasons, Sextus does not characterize the Academics in terms of a priori arguments; he just says that they are the ones who deny that it is possible to get the truth. Perhaps if Sextus were familiar with our notion of a prioricity, but not too familiar, he might think that only a priori objections could result in modalized judgments. As it is, he doesn't specify what kinds of objections or judgments the Academic has, only that they arrive at a denial of possibility.[24] But if the denial of possibility is the differentia of the dogmatic skeptic, as Sextus says, then Burnyeat has,

24. The Academics "*apephênanto mê dunaton einai touto* [*to alêthes*] *katalêphthênai*" PH I.i

after all, accused him of being a dogmatic. For his claim was that anxiety and "immense worry" would be the result of anything less than a modalized judgment of *epokhê*. "Still less should he be wondering whether *in general* contrary claims are equally balanced. For if it is a *real possibility* for him that [contrary claims] are not [equally balanced], that means it is a *real possibility* that there are answers to be found ... [emphasis added]" and this rules out tranquillity. The belief Burnyeat has uncovered, that lets the Pyrrhonian move from *epokhê* to *ataraxia*, is the belief that it is not possible for there to be a one-sided argument, and consequently that it is not possible for answers to be found. Perhaps Burnyeat has in mind some distinction between possibilities and "real possibilities", but without further argument on Burnyeat's part the distinction, like his exposed Skeptic, is Academic.

So Burnyeat's Pyrrhonian has turned out to have ended his enquiry with what is actually a belief that, e.g., to every argument there is an equal argument opposed. And so his Pyrrhonian's tranquillity is not actually consistent with suspension and continued enquiry into the truth, but only with limited suspension, combined with a dogmatic judgment in which that suspension is expressed.

But the fact that Burnyeat's Pyrrhonian Skeptic has turned out to be neither a Skeptic nor a Pyrrhonian should, I think, give us further reason to reject the traditional interpretation which makes Sextus inconsistent in this way. I want to do this, by seeing how one could deny each of Burnyeat's charges of illicit belief. I will present a picture of the Skeptic which I believe defends him from Burnyeat's two charges, and then see whether it is an adequate picture on general grounds.

Let me address the second problem first, because it is the easier, and because Burnyeat uses the second problem in order to cut off an escape route from the first problem—an escape-route that, in fact, I will not choose, but one which we should not think he has blocked when we turn later to inspecting the first problem.

Burnyeat thinks that continued unsuccessful enquiry is wholly incompatible with tranquillity.[25] He poses three options for the Skeptic: either the enquiry has been successful in leading to beliefs;

25. The enquiries of the dogmatists—whether Stoics or Academics—lead to beliefs about dogmatical matters, which they believe are true. I call this a successful enquiry without considering whether the beliefs arrived at are in fact true. Consequently I call the Skeptic's enquiries unsuccessful just in that they do not lead to the holding of beliefs about dogmatical matters.

or the enquiry has actually (i.e., despite the Skeptic's claim) been discontinued, and ended in a claim that truth is unattainable; or the Skeptic is not actually tranquil. The Skeptic, on the other hand, claims to be still enquiring, claims not to have arrived at beliefs (whether positive or negative), and claims to be tranquil. It is not clear whether, on reflection, the Skeptic would want to say that his experience is an instance of a general pattern, i.e., it is not clear whether the Skeptic would want to claim that anyone who enquires as he does will be tranquil. And this is not clear for at least two reasons: first, because it is not clear whether the Skeptic wants to make a claim that look so much like a scientific generalization over a natural kind; and second because, even in his own case, it is not clear whether he would want to give the report of his experience the look of a causal report. Talk of suspension's being the cause of tranquillity, talk of this being a theorem of human psychology—all of this must sit uneasily on the Skeptic. It is presumably to forestall such entanglements that he compares tranquillity's following suspension to a shadow's following a body.[26] The analogy's point, presumably, is that one can have any number of theories about what bodies really are, about whether light is a type of body or a disposition of bodies or perhaps an activity, about whether shadows should be counted in the inventory of what is, and so on: but no-one would honestly deny that it seems to them that shadows follow bodies, and unless one is a committed dogmatist there seems to be absolutely nothing troubling or problematical about this. His experience has been like that.

So the Skeptic is not making any sort of grandiose claim about psychology; only reporting on his own experience. But even if he were to drop all talk of "following", and merely point out that these two states coexist in him, he would still be at odds with Burnyeat. For Burnyeat, unlike the Skeptic, has made a psychological claim about all human beings (at least), and the claim is that it is impossible for anyone both to suspend and to be tranquil.

One might wonder, in general, why Burnyeat might believe this claim, how he would want to support it, and what he would consider evidence against it. I would like to offer, on the Skeptic's behalf, an analysis of why someone might come to believe Burnyeat's claim, and then offer some arguments against it. We

26. It may be worth noting that this word, "*parakolouthein*", is used by Plato of shadows and reflections following bodies, at Sophist 266c.

know that the Skeptic can imagine someone's believing Burnyeat's claim, because we know that there was a time when the Skeptic himself believed Burnyeat's claim. Of course, this has to be read *sensu diviso*: in his youth, the person who would later become a Skeptic believed what, as a mature Skeptic, he would no longer believe. This we know from PH I. 12, the Skeptic's genealogy. Certain people were disturbed by the anomaly in things, and began to inquire about truth, in hopes of attaining tranquillity. Straight off this summary gives us one direction of a biconditional: the proto-Skeptics believed (the future participle is reasonably so construed) that attaining truth would give them tranquillity. Perhaps they thought the truth is all that anyone ever needs, or perhaps they felt it was all that they needed, given what they had; whether they thought it generally sufficient or not, they at least thought: if we had the truth, we would have tranquillity. The second direction—that they believed that only attaining the truth would give them tranquillity—becomes clear when we take a closer look at the first half of the summary. The proto-Skeptics found things anomalous, and found this fact, in turn, a source of unease. They believed, that is, that not having the truth is irreducibly disturbing; that no matter what else one might have in the way of tranquillity, if one did not have the truth one could not be tranquil. This is the second half of the biconditional, and it is the belief that Burnyeat shares with the proto-Skeptics.[27]

This might seem like a misdiagnosis of the proto-Skeptics' plight. It might seem that I have replaced a first order worry with a second order worry, distorting the proto-Skeptic by so doing. Sextus says that the proto-Skeptic was disturbed by the anomaly in things; doesn't this just mean that he worried about, e.g., whether some sentences involving predicates like "bald" violate the law of excluded middle? He thinks, e.g., that there is good reason to abandon the law, but that this would vitiate logic as he conceives of it, and this anomaly is the source of his discomfort; his constant reflection on both sides of the argument, and his vacillation between the two, are the disturbance. The proto-Skeptic has a great number of these first-order worries; why think that he wor-

27. The idea that tranquillity requires a successful completion of enquiry is also found among the Dogmatists; compare Epicurus' statement at the beginning of Ep. Pyth. (DL X.85) that the study of physics has no other goal than tranquillity and firm conviction (*mê allo ti telos ê per ataraxian kai pistin bebaion*).

ries, in addition, about his not (yet) having gotten at the truth? Why claim that the source of his discomfort is reflection on his own position, instead of individual puzzles and contradictions?

I myself do not claim this; but I claim that Sextus claims it. That is, I think that his diagnosis focuses on the second-order worries, and is not about first-order worries. In fact, this distinction is at the heart of the matter; because what the Skeptic maintains is that there is nothing intrinsically disturbing about first-order puzzles and contradictions whatsoever, unless one has the additional belief that one's inability to solve them is in itself worrisome. This additional belief, that one's inability to resolve the puzzles is a bad thing in that it rules out the attainment of tranquillity, is like those additional beliefs that Sextus says make most people miserable, at times when they would otherwise be only moderately affected (PH I.30). In this case, however, there is not even any residual cause of unavoidable disturbance. All of the proto-Skeptic's disturbance, it turns out, was second-order; all of it was caused by the belief that only truth could lead to tranquillity. The Skeptic still faces the contradictions and puzzles he met as an aspiring dogmatist, but contemplating them is now a source of tranquillity for him.[28]

But this should make it clear that Burnyeat has not discovered some sort of hidden flaw in the Skeptic's claim that tranquillity follows on suspension; rather, Burnyeat just believes something that the Skeptic once believed, and no longer does. And the Skeptic is aware of having once held the belief, and aware that he presently does not. Burnyeat himself still holds this belief, and in consequence he also accuses the Pyrrhonian, despite his conscious protestations, of being a Dogmatic Skeptic—remember that it was the claim that tranquillity is incompatible with continued enquiry that led to the claim that the Pyrrhonian must deny even the possibility of attaining truth.[29] But this means that Burnyeat's overall

28. Indeed, the shift in the Skeptic's beliefs about the relation between suspension and tranquillity is in some ways parallel to what Epicurus describes in KD 18: the greatest mental pleasure is produced by reflecting on those very things—i.e. the equipollence of arguments, the Skeptic would say—that once caused us alarm. Of course, it is crucial for Epicurus that one now has attained the truth about things; he thinks that only possession of the truth can overcome one's superstitious fears. But the Skeptic would presumably reply that the fears themselves were based on beliefs; what is needed are not more beliefs but fewer.

29. It occurs to me that "despite his conscious protestations", like Sextus' "*kath' hoiondêpote tropon*" (PH I.8), requires explaining. It can either go with the Pyrrhonian, who protests that he is not an Academic, or with Burnyeat, who protests that he is not accusing the Pyrrhonian of negative dogmatism.

claim is a dogmatic one, in the modern, pejorative sense; he does not offer new arguments that his opponent had failed to consider, he just flatly maintains what his opponent consciously denies, and flatly denies what his opponent consciously maintains. In particular, he maintains that the Pyrrhonian must have ended his enquiry, despite Sextus' care in insisting that he still inquires; and he flatly denies that anyone can both continue enquiring unsuccessfully and be tranquil, despite Sextus' repeated insistence that continued unsuccessful enquiry is exactly what does lead to tranquillity, at least in his own case.

My inclination is to think that we should take Sextus' word for it, since he is presumably in a better position to judge. Nevertheless, it seems that many students of Skepticism have been persuaded by Burnyeat's position, and so it is at least worth asking why it strikes so many as plausible. I assume that the answer has to do with their own attitudes towards philosophical enquiry; they themselves simply feel uneasy until they have fixed on something as the truth, until, in Burnyeat's words, their "questing thoughts [have] come to a state of rest or equilibrium". But it seems to me equally possible that someone could simply enjoy doing philosophy as an activity in itself. It is striking, indeed, that most historians of philosophy deny that Sextus can truly be tranquil, when they are engaged in what is in many ways the same day-by-day activity: comparing the epistemologies of the Stoics and Epicureans, interpreting bits of Parmenides, considering Peripatetic arguments, coming up with counter-arguments, and so on. I should have thought that people in this business would all immediately agree that Sextus' life—during which he produced the equivalent of four Loeb volumes in his spare time—was a truly enviable one. After all, he was not forced to write by pressures to publish or concerns about tenure; he simply enjoyed doing what he did. And the remaining criticism—"yes, but he cannot have been tranquil, because he never got anywhere; he never made up his mind"—simply repeats the very belief that the proto-Skeptic had, which, Sextus tells us, prevented him from true tranquillity.

Now I would like to turn to Burnyeat's first charge, that the Skeptic's suspension of belief, his move from *isostheneia* to *epokhê*, involves him in the sort of belief that he claims not to have. By articulating the charge, we can get a sense of the primary ways in which it might be denied. I take it that it runs roughly like this: the

Skeptic concludes that, e.g., to every argument there is opposed an equal argument (or any other of the ephectic formulae), and this conclusion is based on arguments; but a conclusion based on arguments is the sort of belief that the Skeptic claims not to have. It seems to me that there are three parts to this claim: 1) that the Skeptic reaches a conclusion (summarized in the ephectic formulae); 2) that the conclusion is based on arguments; and 3) that maintaining conclusions arrived at in this way is not consistent with the Skeptic's claim not to have beliefs.

It is my understanding that Frede's defense of the Skeptic consists in a denial of 3), with a consequent, but secondary, denial of 2). That is, he argues that the Skeptic does not deny having quotidian beliefs, only systematic, scientific beliefs about the true nature of things, beliefs that offer to depict reality in some elevated way. Such beliefs would be elevated both in that they claim to contain a deeper insight into reality, and in that they claim to be arrived at or justified in accordance with systematic, scientific canons and criteria. And Frede argues that the Skeptic's formulae of suspense do not pretend to express beliefs of this kind; they are not claims to a deeper insight, just records of how things strike the Skeptic—in particular, records of how his investigations into Dogmatical debates have affected him. This is a direct denial of 3); it seems to me to involve a denial of 2) as well, at least in that Frede would presumably deny, on the Skeptic's behalf, that the formulae are based on the arguments, if that were interpreted as a claim that they are justified by the arguments, or that they are, e.g., conclusions that really do follow from those arguments. For, among other things, that would involve the acceptance of certain canons of consequence, which in general themselves are disputed. So I assume that just as Frede would deny that the Skeptical formulae are beliefs of the elevated kind unacceptable to the Skeptic, so, I suspect, he would deny that the Skeptic believes them on the basis of arguments, if that meant that the Skeptic's beliefs followed from or were justified by the argument in any of the ways specially sanctioned by the dogmatists.

I would like to try another route, to wit, denying the first part of the charge. I do this, not because I think that Frede's defense will not work, but because I think that there are more problems to be solved with Skepticism than are solved by his defense alone, and that denying the first part of the charge might help us to solve them. So far as I know, nothing about my strategy requires a rejection of Frede's defense, and it may well be right. But I hope to show that it can be supplemented to good effect.

To deny the first part of Burnyeat's charge means to deny that the ephectic formulae are conclusions. I do not mean by this that they are not what we would technically call conclusions, according to some theory of proof; that route was sketched out above in the denial of 2). Rather I mean something very straightforward: the Skeptic doesn't come to, or arrive at, a suspension of belief, for the very simple reason that that is where he has always been, and indeed where he started. If we take seriously the distinction between evident and non-evident things, and the Skeptic's autobiography of I. 12, we should conclude that before the Skeptic ever became a Skeptic, he was already in a state of suspension about the nonevident things, i.e., about the things about which he wanted to find out the truth. After all, let us say that you or I were faced with a question about a non-evident affair, as for instance the odd-or-evenness of the number of stars, or the existence of seven sequential sevens in the decimal expansion of pi. Surely on any account of rationality, or by any of the dogmatic or even popular accounts of method, the thing for us to do is to approach the enquiry with a completely open mind, without any prejudicial beliefs about the matter. This is not merely a prescription of philosophic method; it is also enjoined on us at the start of, e.g., a judicial investigation; and its place in legal procedure reflects a fairly popular picture of the right way to investigate something non-evident. Of course, it is not part of the popular picture that we should be open-minded about any question laid before us, e.g., whether I am now sitting in front of a fire-place. We are not, in general, enjoined to be open-minded about such a question, as we are when we are sworn onto a jury; although this is not because there is enshrined in the popular picture any explicit distinction between evident and nonevident. Nevertheless, although we are not universally enjoined to approach everything with an open mind, nor given any rigorous account of which questions we should and should not approach in this way, still it is usually considered that this is the right way to investigate something that is not obvious, or about which one does not know at first what to say. Thus I think it is reasonable to imagine that the proto-Skeptic, too, approached the question of non-evident things in this way. Indeed, he will have had not only popular enjoinders to do so, but as well the universal agreement of the dogmatic schools to which he looked for enlightenment.

But if this is so, then why should we think of the suspension that the Skeptic now professes as in any sense a conclusion? It is not a new development; it is just the very same state in which the earnest, open-minded student began. His mind was unprejudiced, exactly in the center of the issue, ready to be persuaded by one side or the other. It is still there, and still open to that persuasion. It is not, in Burnyeat's phrase, "paralyzed" by the presence of countervailing arguments; quite the opposite, it is simply unmoved by either side. None of the arguments, whether propounded by the dogmatists or invented by the Skeptic himself, has the kind of persuasive force that, e.g., one's own hunger does. All of them leave him unmoved. He is still open to any persuasion that might move him from his position, and indeed, he is still looking for it; he is still in the process of searching.

This seems to me to be the right way to look at the Skeptic's suspension; it is not in any sense a conclusion, not even in the sense of being the result of his examination of arguments, where "result" might have a looser sense than that suggested by the terminology of conclusions, consequence, and so on.

In all respects then, except one crucial one to be discussed, the Skeptic believes now exactly what he believed before he was a Skeptic. We should not imagine that he was once a complacent Stoic or Epicurean, who suddenly had his complacency shattered; rather, he was someone who had a variety of beliefs about evident things, and lived a conventional life, but did not know what to think about the non-evident things—just like the mature Skeptic.

This conservative or inertial picture seems to me crucial in explaining the point with which this section began, namely the question of how the Skeptic can have a conception of the end. For the Skeptic does proclaim an end, and yet one would have thought that his own investigation of dogmatic theories about the end would have left him with the impression that there was as much to be said for this conception of the end as against it, and so with each rival conception. But that is not what Sextus does. Instead, he happily asserts that the end is tranquillity; but it must be emphasized that his actual words are "and we still say", or "and we say even now" (*akhri nun*) that the end is tranquillity.[30] And the next sentence offers an explanation: "For [the Skeptic] began to philosophize in order to become tranquil...", and then goes on to tell the story familiar from PH I.6, about how the desire for tranquillity led to a search for truth, and how the Skeptic found tranquillity without finding truth. The chain of thought, apparently, is this: our end, even now, is tranquillity, for that was our end before we began our investigation into non-evident and anomalous things. This belief that tranquillity is the end was part of the proto-Skeptic's stock of beliefs, and the mature Skeptic inherits it unscathed by his enquiries into non-evident things.

My suggestion, then, is that we see the Skeptic's advocacy of tranquillity as the end as just an instance of the conservation of his pre-Skeptical and proto-Skeptical position. He started with a variety of beliefs about things such as the religious customs of his culture and the rules of his craft, and with a belief about the end which he still professes (*phamen akhri nun*) and with a general commitment to being open-minded about nonevident things. Each of these he retains.

Two points need further attention. First, how is the notion that the Skeptic's suspension is an inheritance from his proto-Skeptical days consistent with the language of following and succession, and the apparently diachronic story that Sextus repeatedly tells, in which equipollence of arguments leads to suspension which then leads to belief? Second, if the Skeptic now believes just what he believed before, and suspends judgment on just those things on which he suspended it before, then what after all did happen to make him a Skeptic, instead of an anxious proto-Skeptic? What was that event which he compares to Apelles' exasperated cast at the canvas?

As to the language of following and succession, it will come as no news to my readers that "first" is said in many ways, and accordingly so is "next" and "after that". And although it was a well-known dogmatist who first pointed it out, what he pointed out was not a bit of dogmatism, but just normal usage. So when Sextus says (PH I.8) that from the Skeptical ability we come through equipollence

30. It is striking that there is no other positive use of the phrases "*akhri nun*" or "*mekhri nun*" in Sextus' works. All of the others (see Janacek's Index s.vv.) are negative, e.g. "up to this point, no agreement has been found". In the other instances, what is conserved is a lack of belief, an irresolution; here alone is some positive claim sustained through out time.

first to *epokhê* and then after that to tranquillity, we do not need to read this as a diachronic claim. The only sense in which the Skeptic arrives at a new state of *epokhê* on any issue, is the sense in which I come to a new state of ignorance on hearing of a new question. Yesterday I knew neither that there was a galaxy called "Andromeda", nor how much it weighed; today I know that there is such a galaxy, and do not know how much it weighs. In some sense my current ignorance of its weight is a development, different from my earlier ignorance of its weight. In the same sense, we might want to say that the Skeptic arrives at *epokhê* in respect to matters that he had never heard of or considered; but this is again not the sort of conclusion to *epokhê* via arguments that Burnyeat had in mind.

There is some other language that is harder to read as non-temporal, and this is in the Skeptic's genealogy and autobiography (PH I. 12, 26, 29). Indeed, by talking throughout about the proto-Skeptic, I have been committing myself to a diachronic account of at least this much. So I take it that in respect to one belief, at least, the proto-Skeptic and the Skeptic must differ. And this will be precisely that second-order belief, that one must grasp the truth before one can become tranquil, which the proto-Skeptic believed and the Skeptic no longer does.

In this one respect, then, the Skeptic has changed his mind. But he needn't do it on the basis of any arguments. For his tranquillity is presumably as evident to him as his hunger is; he needs no special license to conclude that he is tranquil. And so once he finds himself tranquil, and still no further along in his search for truth, he has two evident propositions that he can combine into a rejection of his initial belief that tranquillity is incompatible with continued searching. It is just plain to him, that he is still searching, and that he is tranquil; and observing this he rejects the belief that he had as a proto-Skeptic. One still might wonder, however, how he could come to be tranquil before he rejected that belief. For it was that belief that, in fact, was the cause of his disturbance. No anomaly, no equipollence of argument by itself is disturbing; that is the lesson of the Skeptic's success. But how could he attain that success without rejecting the belief, and how could he reject the belief before he attained the success?

I think that the same well-known dogmatist helps us out here too; for just as knowledge is said in two ways, so is belief: one can have a belief that one is not actively using. And it is not the mere having of the second order belief that prevents one from being tranquil, it is the using of this belief, the contemplation of it and of one's own epistemic situation, that leads to distress. So even during the time that the proto-Skeptic still had the belief that tranquillity requires certainty, he might sometime find himself at the end of his day's investigations into non-evident things and realize that he was feeling utter tranquillity, despite his still searching. And perhaps after landing in this position a few times it would occur to him that this was the position that he was in, and that it was a position that he had believed it impossible to be in. At this point he would move from having but not using the belief to not even having it.

So I argue that the only way in which the Skeptic differs from the proto-Skeptic is with regard to this second-order belief. The Skeptic does not arrive at reasoned conclusions to *epokhê*; *epokhê* was there from the start. He does conclude that, contrary to his earlier second-order belief, tranquillity is consistent with a continued search. But this conclusion is the result of only that sort of introspection that Burnyeat wants to attribute to him in any case—he does not need reasons to believe that he is tranquil, any more than he needs reasons to believe that he is hungry.

I conclude, then, that the Skeptic can claim without equivocation or bad faith that he is actively searching for the truth about things sought according to philosophy, that he has not found them nor declared them unfindable, and that his search is consistent with his having attained his professed end of tranquillity. I have tried to offer arguments for all of these conclusions; I am not equally satisfied with all of them, but I find them more satisfactory than the arguments to which they are opposed.

III. THE SKEPTIC'S RESPONSE TO THE THIRD CHARGE

We have now spent some time examining the structure of the Skeptic's doctrine of the end, and seeing how it can defend itself from the first two charges leveled against it. With these structures clarified, we can now proceed to the third question with which we started, namely that of the relation between the Skeptic's search for truth and his end of tranquillity.

Our challenge to the Skeptic is to show us how his search for truth, his activity as a Skeptic, is related to his end of tranquillity. Since tranquillity is his end, and an end is that for the sake of which everything else is done or contemplated (a significant addition in this connection), we can assume that whatever the Skeptic does is done for the sake of tranquillity. So in particular, he must be seeking for the truth for the sake of tranquillity. And as our previous discussion suggested, this should mean that truth contributes to tranquillity, in one of the ways specified above. But it seems central to the Skeptic's position, that truth in fact does not contribute to tranquillity; the Skeptic's lack of success in his search for truth has neither prevented his attainment of tranquillity, nor caused him to abandon the search as irrelevant to tranquillity. The search for truth does not seem to be for the sake of tranquillity, in the normal sense of "for the sake of'. One answer to this dilemma is attributed to a group of Skeptics whose relation to Sextus is quite unclear. Commenting on the *phônê* "*panti logôi logon ison antikeitai*", Sextus says:

> Some also utter the *phônê* in the following way: "*panti logôi logon ison antikeisthai*" [the infinitive for the indicative], intending to give the injunction "to every argument which establishes a point dogmatically, *let us oppose* an argument which investigates dogmatically, equal to the former in respect of persuasion and dissuasion, and conflicting therewith"; for they mean their words to be addressed to the Skeptic, using the infinitive form "to be opposed" in place of the imperative "let us oppose". And they address this injunction to the Skeptic lest haply, being led astray by the Dogmatist, he may give up the Skeptic search, and, through precipitancy, be balked of the tranquillity that appears to them, which they believe arises in consequence with *epokhê* about everything (as we said above).[31] (PH I.205)

This quotation relates tranquillity and the search for truth through the skeptical activity of opposing arguments. One must search for truth, and so compare arguments, because otherwise one may be falsely persuaded by bad Dogmatical arguments and so

31. The last parenthetical comment again urges us to understand the "*epokhê peri pantôn*" in light of the restriction of "*panta*" in PH I. 198, referred to above.

come to partake of dogmatical views oneself, thereby losing tranquillity.[32] The concern, I take it, is not that one would come to have new beliefs; for on my account the Skeptic must be doing this all day long, as any of us does. Rather, the concern is that one would come to have new beliefs of a certain kind, held for a certain reason, namely on the basis of Dogmatical arguments (see above, "to every argument that establishes something dogmatically..."). If, after opposing to this first lot an equal and opposite lot of Dogmatical arguments, one found that one had nevertheless acquired a new belief, then this would provide some evidence that one had not acquired it, and did not hold it, on the basis of arguments; one merely felt compelled by how things struck one, and so believed it on that basis. And having arrived at it in this way, one would not feel that one then had to assent to, e.g., its deductive consequences, merely because they were deductive consequences (under some set of rules or another), unless those also struck you as independently compelling.

It is not clear whether this would be Sextus' own answer, because he explicitly attributes this reading of the *phônê* to "*tines*", who are presumably Skeptics, but may differ from Sextus. It may be that he has the same group of Skeptics in mind at PH I.30, when he says that some well-known skeptics have added to the end that he professes, the further end of *epokhê* in enquiries. Bury, comparing DL IX.107, supposes that these further skeptics are the ones mentioned there as "the followers of Timon and Aenesidemus". But that identification may not be right; for these latter skeptics only profess one end, *epokhê*, and then say that *ataraxia* follows on it like a shadow. Tranquillity, in other words, is not an end for them at all; they structure their pursuits in order to attain suspension, and then tranquillity comes of its own, like an *epigennêma*. This may represent a third and different way of answering the question that I am now asking, about the relation between tranquillity and the end-directed activities of the skeptic. In any case, the skeptics mentioned at PH I.30 profess a complex end; *epokhê* is something that they added (*prosethêkan*) to the ends professed by Sextus. So they may not be the "followers of Timon and Aenesidemus" mentioned

32. This makes clear the double characterization of the Skeptics; they are both the people who continue to search, as PH I. 1-4 has it, and the people who share in an antithetical capacity, as PH I.8-11 has it. I take it that the latter is the more essential characteristic, the former the more accidental.

at DL IX. 107, and neither of these are necessarily the same as the "*tines*" who warn against being diverted by Dogmatists in PH I.204. It is difficult to sort out how many strains of Skepticism are in play here, and how they are related to Sextus. I am inclined to suppose that a more useful route of resolution lies in the articulation of Sextus' end. I have spoken so far as though that were simply tranquillity; in fact, as Sextus makes clear at several places, it is *ataraxia* in respect to matters of dogmatic subtlety, and "moderate affection" (*metriopatheia*) in respect of compulsory things.[33] Since moderate affection in compulsory things is a part of his end, it is perfectly consistent for him to undertake activities or contemplation for the sake of moderate affection. But here it seems to me there is an ambiguity in this characterization, that can make *metriopatheia* look more consistent with the traditional interpretation, or with the revisionist interpretation. "The Skeptic strives for moderate affection in compulsory things" may mean either

> 1): there are certain things that are compulsory, and the Skeptic strives to experience only a moderate amount of suffering when in them;
>
> or 2): the Skeptic strives to experience only a moderate amount of those things in which suffering is compulsory.

On the rabid view, the Skeptic must treat every external event as beyond their ability to intervene (since intervention would involve them in prohibited beliefs) and thus compulsory; the cart is going to hit them, the precipice is going to yawn before their feet, and the Skeptic will make no move to avoid these external blows. Instead, the rabid skeptic will simply aim to control their own internal reactions to these external affairs. This first version goes hand in hand with the picture of the Skeptic striving to live his life as though viewing a film, whose gruesome scenes can be made less alarming to the viewer by constant reminders that it is only a film. The external is fixed and compulsory; only one's own internal attitudes are within one's control (again, it is striking how often the traditional interpretation of the Skeptic attributes to him large quantities of quasi-Stoic dogma).

On the second version, the Skeptic recognizes that there are

33. PH I.25, 30; PH III.235-6; AM XI.162

certain external events which, once encountered, are likely to result in internal suffering, e.g. being hit by carts. And in some sense the suffering that ensues is compulsory, not voluntary as are the self-inflicted sufferings of Dogmatists. When one is hit by a cart, the suffering that ensues is not the result of philosophical beliefs—or at any rate, not all of it is, and those parts of it that are (e.g. an Epicurean's concern that by being in pain they are now experiencing something truly evil) the Skeptic is well-positioned to avoid. But since there will remain a residue of non-dogmatic suffering, necessitated by the external event, the Skeptic has reason to avoid events of this kind. And indeed he follows ordinary life in avoiding things of this sort—and the attempt now can include both the avoidance of external events, as well as the avoidance of excessive, philosophically-induced internal reactions to them. It may be objected to me that "*katênenkasmena*" means necessitated things, non-contingent things, or as Bury translates it, "unavoidable things"; how then can I speak of the Skeptic taking action to avoid them? This objection seems to me to founder on the sorts of examples Sextus uses; death may in some sense be necessary or unavoidable, but shivering and feeling thirst certainly are not.[34] They are only the necessary consequences of being in extremely cold or dry situations; and those are surely the sort of situations that one can avoid, and whose avoidance is prescribed by ordinary life.

It seems quite likely that a better grasp of the truth would allow us to avoid these sorts of situations more effectively. Right now, we are able to avoid the suffering brought on by dogmatic beliefs, because we avoid dogmatic beliefs; and to do this we do not need to have attained the truth. But the truth might itself be very useful to the end of moderating one's suffering; and this is part of the Skeptic's end as well. E.g., the Skeptic tries to avoid becoming ill. But this might be easier if more were known about medicine and diseases; so the search for the truth about medicine (and whatever other truths may be useful to its discovery) is sensibly connected to the goal of experiencing only moderate suffering in compulsory things, i.e. things in which the suffering is not the result of Dogmatic philosophical beliefs.

Imagine, on the contrary, feeling that you were not really justified in wanting to have two children—that you couldn't really

34. PH I. 29

want two children in any deep way—until you had settled the issue between Zermelo-Fraenkel numbers and Von Neumann numbers. Imagine feeling that until you had adopted one of these, and then adopted everything that followed from it, the whole business of numbers was an unjustified and dangerous mess, better to be avoided altogether—and with it all thoughts of having two, or for that matter zero, children.

This is not the Skeptic's position; rather it is the position of those Dogmatists who insist that the Skeptic must have theoretical opinions if he is to be able to live any life at all. This is the attitude that provokes Sextus' comment, at AM X1.165, that the Skeptic does not live his life by philosophical argumentation, but by the unphilosophical observance of ordinary life. Unfortunately, Sextus has historically been met by the reply that if he does use numbers, then he must be committed to some metaphysics of mathematics or another—merely the same old dogmatic assumptions recycled.

One cannot, I think, understand Sextan skepticism until one can conceive of an attitude towards philosophical truth that makes the attainment of the true theory of everything utterly vital; truly worth life itself. One must imagine oneself in a context in which people genuinely believe that until you know whether the Von Neumann or the Zermelo-Fraenkel set-theoretical construction of numbers is correct, you are more miserable than someone being tortured on the rack; and if you should be wrong about your belief then you have committed an act as foul as that of eating your parents' corpses. This is not merely rhetoric for the Greeks; it is standard Stoic doctrine, and many people actually seem to have felt this way. It may be hard for us now to believe that people could view philosophy in that way, but many ancient philosophers were maniacs, pure and simple, utter fanatics. And that mania is exactly what Sextus means by the term "dogmatism".

Now originally the proto-dogmatists and proto-skeptics were in agreement about the overwhelming importance of philosophy. They all believed that life as commonly lived is unacceptably chaotic and unsystematic, and that a completely comprehensive and explanatory theory of everything was necessary before life could be livable at all. For some time, the proto-dogmatists and proto-skeptics followed the same track and had the same experiences—they looked at the rival schools and systems, and studied the different technical philosophies more and more intensely. But despite the fact that the Stoics, Epicureans, Peripatetics and so on all claimed to have developed complete, consistent and perfected systems that explained everything, including their rivals' mistakes, our young students could not help but find that there are problems with each of them, that none of them offer the universal certainty and clarity that was their original goal. And now the crisis comes; now the undifferentiated proto-dogmatists and proto-skeptics diverge and develop into their adult forms. For some of these people, still feeling that they can only live with the assurance of a universal system, simply choose to believe that Stoicism, say, has the truth. They have made the stakes too high not to choose one or another; they truly believe that they cannot live until then, that they cannot engage in life unless it has been sanitized of every possible anomaly, until it is one chain of consistency from beginning to end. So much depends upon this decision, that they subscribe to a dogmatical system with a violent desire, and a sort of identification with it; they are not merely persuaded by it, they willfully choose to believe it. Now, at last, they can have their two children, now that they have convinced themselves that they have the correct theory of number; but it may come as no surprise that any attack on that theory will be about as welcome as an attack on their own offspring.

Such is the making of dogmatists; starting from the belief that the anomaly in things is unlivable, and that their whole lives depend on the attainment of truth, they willfully and rashly opt for one of a number of flawed systems, and then defend the system that they adopt as though their lives depended on it.

Meanwhile, the skeptic for one reason or another has had a different experience. When confronted with the problems and flaws in each of the systematic philosophies, he has simply been unwilling to queer the results arbitrarily, to engage in the kind of self-deception that would be required for him to embrace, let's say, Platonic forms as the foundation of everything, pretending that it was free of problems. The perfect system has always been his goal, but he is unwilling to settle for anything less than the real article, and nothing on offer fills the bill. But then he realizes a funny thing. He realizes that he may have been wrong about the stakes to begin with. It may be that a livable life is attainable, without having attained (or telling yourself that you have attained) the final theory of everything. He may even come to realize, that he can have two children before he has mastered set theory. He may still find that life as commonly lived is chaotic and unsystematic, but perhaps not unbearably so; and in fact, it is less chaotic than the contortions and gyrations demanded by allegiance to the professional schools. The thing that really mattered to him all along—a good life—seems now not to depend on the possession of the ultimate truth in the way it once seemed. And this realization brings with it an immense sense of tranquillity; remember that until that moment the proto-skeptic, like the proto-dogmatists, had felt that life without the ultimate truth was unbearable. Of course, the perfect system would still be nice to have. For one thing, there is still some anomaly in things, and perhaps the perfect system would actually allow us to avoid it without forcing us to accept more anomaly in other parts, as all of the current pretenders do. And for another thing, truth itself might just be a delightful thing in itself to contemplate and think about, especially once the search for it is no longer distorted by the belief that all of our practical goals must wait on its discovery. It seems possible—at least it cannot be ruled out—that the desire for truth is just as natural to people as any other desire—or perhaps not to everyone, but just to certain people, i.e., the ones who are of such a nature as to become philosophers of the dogmatic or skeptical kind.[35] For these reasons, and perhaps for others, the skeptic continues to search for the truth according to philosophy, and continues thinking about the claims of the different schools, and fully accepts the possibility that this search, so far unsuccessful, might eventually succeed.

But meanwhile, having shaken off this nightmare that the ultimate truth of everything is necessary before life can begin, the skeptic goes back to living as everyone else does, planning to have a certain number of children, or saying that it is true that that is how many he has. He has not abandoned his interest in set theory, but he no longer believes that his whole life depends on the outcome of his enquiries. He doesn't entirely understand the foundations of number theory—nor do the dogmatists, either, although they won't admit it—but he certainly thinks he has two children. And if someone were to argue that there is so much anomaly in our everyday conceptions of numbers that it is possible to deduce from

35. AM I.42 on "*philomathia*"; might this be Sextus himself, or is it merely another implicit quotation?

them the theorem that one equals two, then he may admit this; but it will not change how he will react if one of his two children dies. To say that the skeptic only acts *as if* he believed things, that because he does not subscribe to the theories of the dogmatic schools he is engaged in a charade, is equivalent to supposing that anyone who does not endorse one particular axiomatization of arithmetic as irrefutably true would not really care if they had one child less (or more) than they have.

Here is Sextus' own version of the intellectual biography that I have been sketching out:

> The origin of skepticism is the hope of attaining tranquillity. For certain people, distinguished by their great natures, were disturbed by the anomaly in things, and since they were in doubt about which one they should subscribe to, they began their project of enquiry into truth and falsehood, believing that it was by discovering this that they would find relief from disturbance .... Having begun to study philosophy .... they encountered contradictions of equal weight, and being unable to decide between them, they suspended judgment. But having suspended judgment, there followed, as it happened, the state of tranquillity with respect to dogmatical issues .... We do not suppose, however, that the skeptic is wholly untroubled, for we grant that he is troubled by things unavoidable .... Hence we say that the skeptic's end is to be wholly untroubled by issues of dogmatical philosophy, and to experience a moderate amount of the unavoidable things.[36]

The typical reaction that philosophers seem to have when confronted with skeptical arguments is the desire to refute them, and attempts to refute skepticism have been getting a fair number of pages in the journals in recent millennia. One of the effects of shifting our view of Sextus Empiricus in the way that I have been advocating is that we no longer need, and may no longer feel the need, to refute him. If we no longer view him as someone trying to block our attempt to hold or express fundamental convictions, then we may not feel that his refutation is the first thing we have to accomplish before we can get on with our lives. All of that may still be true about some other skeptic or some other brand of skepticism, but not about Sextus Empiricus. In Sextus, it is the dogma-

36. PH I.12, I.26, I.29, I.30

tist who insists that we conduct our lives in accordance with an extreme and fanatical program, and the skeptic who gives us back our ability to do what we want.

Bibliography, Updated to 1999

Allen, J. 1990 "The Skepticism of Sextus Empiricus", *Aufstieg und Niedergang der Römischen Welt* II.36.4: 2582–607.

Allen, J. 1993. "Pyrrhonism and Medical Empiricism", *Aufstieg und Niedergang der Römischen Welt* II.37.1: 646–90.

Annas, J., and Barnes, J. 1985. *The Modes of Skepticism: Ancient Texts and Modern Interpretations*. Cambridge: Cambridge University Press.

Barnes, J. 1983 "The Beliefs of a Pyrrhonist", *Elenchos* 4, 1983, pp. 5–43. First printed in *Proceedings of the Cambridge Philological Society* N.S. 28 1982, 1–29; reprinted as Chapter 3 of Burnyeat and Frede 1997.

Barnes, J. 1990. *The Toils Of Skepticism*. Cambridge: Cambridge Univ. Press.

Bett, R. 1994a. "Aristocles on Timon on Pyrrho", *Oxford Studies in Ancient Philosophy 12*.

Bett, R. 1994b. "What did Pyrrho think about the nature of the divine and the good?", *Phronesis* vol. xxxix/3, pp. 303–337.

Bett, R. 1997. *Against the ethicists : (Adversus mathematicos XI)*. Oxford: Clarendon Press.

Bett, R. 1998. "The Sceptics and the Emotions", Chapter 7 of Engberg-Pedersen and Sihvola 1998.

Blank, D. 1998. *Against the grammarians (Adversus mathematicos I)*. Oxford : Clarendon Press.

Brennan, T. 1994. "Criterion and Appearance in Sextus Empiricus", *Bulletin of the Institute of Classical Studies*, vol. 39 pp. 151–169.

Brennan, T. 1996. "Reasonable Impressions in Stoicism", *Phronesis* vol. xli/3 pp. 318–334.

Brennan, T. 1998a. "Pyrrho on the Criterion", *Ancient Philosophy* 18, pp. 417–434.
Brennan, T. 1998b. "The Old Stoic Theory of Emotions", chapter 2 of Engberg-Pedersen and Sihvola 1998.
Brennan, T. 1998c. Review of Bett 1997. *Journal of Hellenic Studies*, 1998
Brennan, T. 2000. "Criterion and Appearance in Sextus Empiricus", *Acta Philosophica Fennica*.
Brittain, C. 1997. Review of Hankinson 1995, *Philosophical Review* vol. 106 no 4 (October 1997), pp. 635–638.
Brittain, C. 2000. *Philo of Larissa*. Oxford : Clarendon Press.
Brochard, V. 1923. *Les Sceptiques Grecs*, (ed. 2). Paris: Librairie Philosophique J. Vrin.
Brunschwig, J. 1988. "Sextus Empiricus on the *kritêrion*: The Skeptic as Conceptual Legatee," pp. 224–43 of Brunschwig 1994.
Brunschwig, J. 1994. *Papers in Hellenistic Philosophy*. Cambridge: Cambridge University Press.
Burnyeat, M. 1980a. 'Can the Sceptic Live his Scepticism?", pp. 20–53 in Schofield et al. 1980; reprinted as pp. 117–148 of Burnyeat 1983; reprinted as Chapter 2 of Burnyeat and Frede 1997.
Burnyeat, M. 1980b. "Tranquillity without a stop: Timon Frag. 68", Classical Quarterly N.S. 30, p. 86–93.
Burnyeat, M. 1983 (ed.). *The Skeptical Tradition*. Berkeley and Los Angeles: University of California Press.
Burnyeat, M. 1984. "The Sceptic in his Place and Time". in Rorty et al. 1984, pp. 225–254. Reprinted as Chapter 4 of Burnyeat and Frede 1997.
Burnyeat, M. and Frede, M. 1997 (eds.). *The Original Sceptics*. Indianapolis: Hackett Publishing Co.
Bury, R. G. 1933. *Sextus Empiricus*. Cambridge: Harvard University Press.

Cottingham, J., Stoothoff, R., and Murdoch, D. 1984 (eds.). *The Philosophical Writings of Descartes*. Cambridge: Cambridge University Press.

Engberg-Pedersen, T. and Sihvola, J. 1998 (eds.). *The Emotions in Hellenistic Philosophy*. Dordrecht: Kluwer Academic Publishers.

Fine, G. 1996. "Scepticism, existence, and belief", *Oxford Studies in Ancient Philosophy* 14, pp. 273–90.
Fogelin, R. J. 1983. "The Tendency of Hume's Skepticism", pp. 397–412 of Burnyeat 1983.
Fogelin, R. J. 1994. *Pyrrhonian Reflections on Knowledge and Justification*. New York : Oxford University Press.

Fowler, D. 1984. "Sceptics and Epicureans", *Oxford Studies in Ancient Philosophy 2*, pp. 237–67.
Frede, M. 1979. "The Skeptic's Beliefs", chapter 10 of Frede 1987. Reprinted as Chapter 1 of Burnyeat and Frede 1997.
Frede, M. 1984. "The Skeptic's Two Kinds of Assent", in Rorty et al. 1984. Reprinted as Chapter 5 of Burnyeat and Frede 1997.
Frede, M. 1987. *Essays in Ancient Philosophy*. Minneapolis: University of Minnesota Press.

Glidden, D. K. 1983. "Skeptic Semiotics", *Phronesis* XXVIH, p. 213–255.
Groarke, L. 1990. *Greek Scepticism: Anti-Realist Trends in Ancient Thought*. Montreal & Kingston: McGill-Queen's University Press.

Hallie, P. 1985. *Sextus Empiricus: Selections from the Main Writings on Scepticism, Man & God*. Indianapolis: Hackett Publishing Co.
Hankinson, R. J. 1995. *The Sceptics*. London & New York: Routledge.
Harman, G. 1986. *Change in View: Principles of Reasoning*. Cambridge, Mass.: The MIT Press.
Heintz, W. 1932. *Studien zu Sextus Empiricus*. Halle (Saale): Max Niemeyer Verlag.
Hiley, D. R. 1988. *Philosophy in Question: Essays on a Pyrrhonian Theme*. Chicago: The University of Chicago Press.
House, D. K. 1980. "The Life of Sextus Empiricus," *Classical Quarterly* 30, pp. 227–38.

Inwood, B. 1985. *Ethics and Human Action in Early Stoicism*. Oxford: Clarendon Press.

Janacek, K. 1972. *Sextus Empiricus' Skeptical Methods*. Prague.

Long, A. A. 1986. *Hellenistic Philosophy*, (ed. 2). Berkeley and Los Angeles: University of California Press.
Long, A. A., and Sedley, D. N. 1987 (eds.). *The Hellenistic Philosophers*. Cambridge: Cambridge University Press.

McPherran, M. 1987. "Skeptical Homeopathy and Self-Refutation". *Phronesis* 32, pp. 290–328.
Morrison, D. 1990. "The Ancient Sceptic's Way of Life". *Metaphilosophy* 21(3), pp. 204–222.

Pentzopolou-Valalas, T. 1988. "L'epoché ou la conquête du phénomène", *Kantstudien* 79, pp. 218–235.

Rorty, R., Schneewind, J. B., and Skinner, Q. 1984 (eds.). *Philosophy in History . Essays on the Historiography of Philosophy*. Cambridge:Cambridge University Press.

Schmitt, C. B. 1983. "The Rediscovery of Ancient Skepticism", in Burnyeat 1983.

Schofield, M., Burnyeat, M. and Barnes, J. 1980 (eds.). *Doubt and Dogmatism: Studies in Hellenistic Epistemology*. Oxford: The Clarendon Press.

Schofield, M., and Striker, G. 1986 (eds.). *The Norms of Nature: Studies in Hellenistic Ethics*. Cambridge: Cambridge University Press.

Sedley, D. 1983. "The Motivation of Greek Skepticism" Chapter 1 of Burnyeat 1983.

Spinelli, E. 1995. *Sesto Empirico Contro gli etici; introduzione, edizione, traduzione e commento*. [Naples] : Bibliopolis.

Striker, G. 1980. "Sceptical Strategies", in Schofield, Burnyeat and Barnes 1980. Reprinted as Chapter 4 of Striker 1996.

Striker, G. 1981. "On the Difference between the Pyrrhonists and the Academics", Phronesis vol. 26, pp. 153–171. Reprinted as Chapter 6 of Striker 1996.

Striker, G. 1983. "The Ten Tropes of Aenesidemus", in Burnyeat 1983. Reprinted as Chapter 5 of Striker 1996.

Striker, G. 1990. "Ataraxia: Happiness as Tranquillity", *Monist* vol. 73, pp. 97–110. Reprinted as Chapter 9 of Striker 1996.

Striker, G. 1996. *Essays in Hellenistic Epistemology and Ethics*. Cambridge: Cambridge University Press.

Stroud, B. 1984. *The Significance of Philosophical Skepticism*. Oxford: The Clarendon Press.

Index